TWENTIETH CE

HEDNESFORD

(Including Hazel Slade, Pye Green, Rawnsley & Wimblebury)

Anthony Hunt

Published by
Mount Chase Press
109 Mount Street, Hednesford, Cannock, Staffs. WS12 4DB
01543 422891

ISBN 978-0-9551382-7-0

Designed and produced by John Griffiths, printed in the UK.

Contents

List of photographs and maps

Acknowledgements

Once again many thanks to all those Cannock library staff whom I pestered throughout the research into this latest book. Also many thanks to all those people who lent photographs over the years. They are as follows:-

J. Baker for **1**; S. Belcher for **7, 8, 83, 85, 86** and **87**; J. Bill for **33**; H. Bird for **61** and **62**; the *Birmingham Post* for **67, 97** and **114**; K. Brown for **75**; M. Cartwright for **32**; Miss Cornwall for **48**; D. Davis for **43** and **134**; Mr. Davies for **57**; E. Dawes for **38, 39** and **40**; W. Edwards for **54**; Mrs. Forrester for **41** and **60**; J. Goucher for **76**; M. Gray for **68**, **100**, **Cover** and **Title page** picture; S. Green for **113**; J. Hartshorn for **58, 88, 90, 92, 93, 94, 95, 96, 101, 103, 112, 115, 116, 117** and **129**; Mrs L. Humphreys (nee Rosson) for **2, 12, 44** and **89**; P. Jarvis for **78** and **79**; M. Kettle for **74, 77, 109** and **122**; J. Latham for **9**; J. Lomas for **123** and **146**; A. Lycett for **121, 127** and **130**; M. McPherson for **22** and **45**; the Museum of Cannock Chase for **42, 46, 53, 73, 80** and **126**; J. Pickerill for **25, 64** and **133**; J. Richards for **99** and **102**; Mrs. S. Smith for **15** and **20**. Many thanks must also go to Tessa Dudley who sold me her vast collection of old Hednesford photographs at such a very reasonable price.

All the photographs used were supplied in good faith, but apologies to anyone whose copyright may have been unintentionally infringed.

Introduction

Having already written *A History of Hednesford and Surrounding Villages* the reader may ask is there any more of the story to be told? A good question. Quite simply the first book dealt with the history of the area, but could not hope to deal with any particular century in great detail and so the twentieth century in particular, when Hednesford and the surrounding area saw its greatest development, was only briefly mentioned. This book aims to rectify that and deals with the growth of the area from 1900 onwards when the area as we know it today really began to expand. The book can also act as a memory guide because time moves so quickly and exact dates soon fade.

Written in diary form it follows all the major events in the town and local villages, Hazel Slade, Pye Green, Rawnsley and Wimblebury, and shows their development from small mining areas to what we know and see today. It names most of the actual streets in the area from their origins as simple country lanes through to their fight to get them tarmaced and paved; a fight which still goes on today. Development largely rests on the initiative of the residents and the book gives some of the life stories of those who played a major part in the area either with their insight and knowledge or just their dogged determination to succeed. You may be surprised to learn that some of those people introduced industries into the area that were national firsts, such as the enamelling and fibre glass process in making household goods or the first paper bag making machinery. Whilst mentioning those people the book also includes stories and memories from residents who knew the area before it grew and I have also included historical notes where relevant. (Here I apologise for not including an index to the book as it would have been far too extensive.)

Coupled with that it will also show how slow some progress was at times, despite the wishes of the people or its desperate need, because the twentieth century saw the growth of bureaucracy and we all know how that can slow down any growth. The one tool that the bureaucrats and planners always had to their advantage to slow progress was the cost of any improvements and readers will be surprised at how costs escalated during the century. Talk of hundreds of pounds soon became thousands and by today's reckoning millions. Following those figures gives an estimation of the rise in the cost of living; an example of which is wage packets for workers. I can remember my father getting £4 a week in the 1940's and we thought he was on a good wage; and my own £39 per month in the early 1960's as a teacher seemed like a fortune!

You may also like to know just how our attitudes have changed over the century. Sunday entertainment was taboo, save for church and its services; shopping hours greatly differed; transport was limited to the very few; even clothing was highly regulated – a far cry from today's free for all! I wonder just how many of us would really call them the "good old days" if we had to go back to those restrictions?

With those things in mind this then seems the ideal time to recap on Hednesford and the surrounding area before any of this started.

A brief historical recap – From its origins in the twelfth century as Haddensford the village remained a backwater until the eighteenth century when the growth of racehorse training began to flourish. Some might argue that it was more famous at that time than it is today as the nobility certainly knew where Hednesford was on the map. However it was still a small village, centred around the Cross Keys Inn (Old Hednesford). Hazel Slade also existed because of its stables, but the other villages were non-existent save for their single farmsteads and name.

The first crucial step on the road to growth was the opening of the railway station in Hednesford in 1859. Used mainly by the racehorse trainers, it was a fair distance from the Cross Keys area. Its positioning was purely financial as the most direct and least costly route between Walsall and Rugeley lay along the valley where Rising Brook stream ran. At the time the only building close to the station was Hednesford Lodge and that, as you can see from the map, was on a country track, not a road.

What would enhance the rapid growth was the demise of the coal industry in South Staffordshire and Shropshire and the need to find more reserves. Hednesford already had coal mines near the Cross Keys, but with the opening of the West Cannock and Cannock and Rugeley mining companies in the late 1860's things really took off. There was one drawback – those mines and the houses for their workers were nowhere near Hednesford. The simple answer was to move the town closer to the mines and so the Hednesford as we know it today began.

Station Street (the lane outside the Anglesey Commercial Hotel) as it was originally called saw the building of shops on a massive scale in the late 1860's and early 1870's. The shops opposite the Anglesey were the first and gradually the line extended down Market Street (its new name) towards Rugeley Road. The Market Hall opened in 1872 to cater for shopkeepers who did not have regular premises; the Post Office had opened its doors in 1862 and saw a huge turnover of customers; Moore's factory began in 1876; and just to prove its growing importance Lloyd's opened a bank in the town closely followed by the Staffordshire Joint Stock Bank.

By 1881 Market Street as we know it today was vibrant with well over fifty shops catering for a population which had rocketed from just 500 in 1860 to over 6,000 in the 1880's. Villages like Wimblebury and Rawnsley, which had not existed, in 1870 suddenly grew when mines were opened close by. Schools had opened in all the villages by 1890 and adult entertainment was catered for at the Public Rooms opened in 1876 and in public houses. Sport was soon organised with many football teams being started by miners and the spiritual side was not forgotten with over twenty chapels or churches having been constructed. Streets were lit by gas lamps and everywhere seemed to be thriving.

But the beginning of a new century does not mean that everything changed and some issues, of necessity, persisted into the next era. In the early 1880's the Government had passed the Electric Lighting Act which called for all local councils to install the new system as soon as it was economically viable. As you will discover during this diary our area rather dragged its feet on the issue, preferring to stay with gas lighting which had prevailed since the 1870's. Hednesford's own gasometers had been installed in Victoria Street and Hednesford had got its first gas street lamps in 1878.

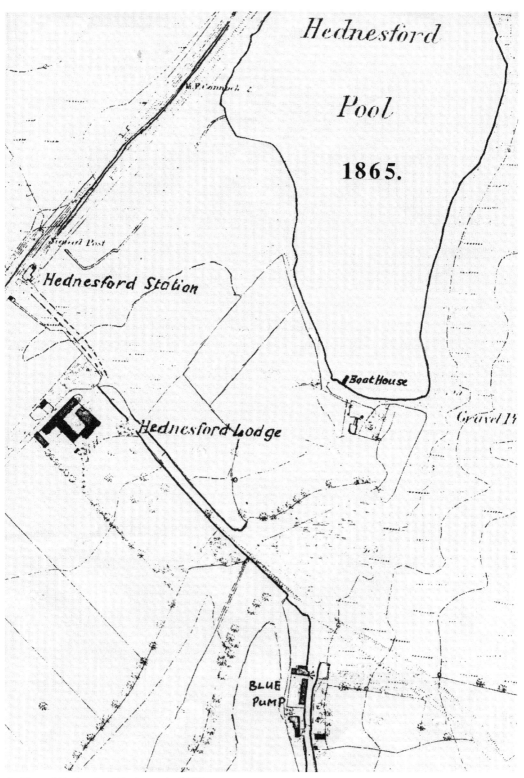

1. Map of Hednesford Pool area in 1865.

Another issue, which is still muted even today, was the possibility of Hednesford having its own local council, completely separate from Cannock. The Local Government Act of 1894 set in motion the idea that Hednesford could apply to be a separate authority and a mass meeting held at the Market Hall that year proposed to break away from Cannock. The area was governed by the Cannock Local Board, but after the Act would become the Urban District Council. The meeting proposed that it was advisable that Hednesford along with Chadsmoor, Rawnsley, Wimblebury and Cannock Wood, together with Pye Green and Green Heath, should become a new authority as "Cannock got its interests attended to more than Hednesford did". Mr. John Cole, a working class member of the executive representing a Hednesford ward, argued, "Having had Cannock rule applied rather vigorously it was about time they had Home Rule at Hednesford". More money was spent on Cannock than anywhere else. Heard this argument before?

But perhaps the most serious issue to go into the next century was one that affected all of the country – the Boer War. What had started out as a disagreement between the Transvaal Government and Britain in early 1899 had escalated into war by the October. Apart from having Hednesford men fighting on the front line Hednesford people showed their generosity by holding many events to raise money for those families affected by the war (the same would happen in future wars). December 13th, 1899 saw a concert held at the Drill Hall in Victoria Street to raise further funds (some £200 had already been donated). Councillor A. Stanley, miners' agent, presided and stated that "families of those affected in the district were being well cared for" and if "other districts were to do their share equally in comparison to the miners and people of the Cannock Chase area there would be sufficient funds in the country to help all the families of fighting troops". During that evening the Volunteer Band, under bandmaster Mr. Cotterell, and various singers entertained the massive audience and another £30 to £40 was raised – a hefty sum in those days!

And so to the twentieth century........

The Century Begins
(1900 - 1909)

1900

January Bradbury Lane Wesleyan Chapel installed its new organ and in the concert to celebrate it Mr. S.J. Stanton played various hymns.

January 21st The annual exhibition of the Hednesford Poultry Show took place in the Drill Hall. This show would continue for many years, finally ending before the Second World War. Hednesford also had its Rabbit Show and it still continues today with three shows held each year with Cannock Wood Community Centre as its headquarters. Rawnsley had its annual Flower Show in the August/September which lasted until 1939.

★Historical note - Many of these shows were a development from the aristocracy who bred animals like rabbits and pigeons for food. In Hednesford and Hazel Slade the Marquis of Anglesey had several rabbit conies, breeding them for food. In 1770 William Cooper ran one in Hednesford and 700 pairs of rabbits were slaughtered each year. An expenses sheet for that year reads:- " 5 men and one boy to help with the slaughter, £16 10s; the keep of three dogs and three ferrets, £2 12s; traps,

2. *Harry Bate, father of Daisy Astle, with rabbit cups.*

£4 5s; expenses, including transport to market, £5 15s;" whilst Cooper had £26 7s for his expenses. The total cost for the one coney was £58 per year, a huge amount for the times.

Miners willingly took up the idea of breeding racing pigeons and keeping other livestock as a distraction from their work down the mines, but purely for entertainment and sport.

February 15th Major R.S. Williamson organised a dinner at the Anglesey Hotel to give a suitable send off to the four local volunteers who had been accepted for the war in South Africa. The four men were Privates W. Perry, J. Buckley, J. Powis and J. Reynolds of Company F of the Volunteer Brigade of the South Staffs. Also present at the meal were the reserve Privates:- J. Langley, J. Bradnick, D. Seabury and J. Kendall. Those four men would join their comrades later in the year.

During the dinner money was raised for the men to help them on their way. A total of £17 12s 9d was raised. Each man would get £1 then; £1 when ready to sail; and the remainder later.

*Interesting to note that the Government grant only provided 35 shillings (£1.75p today) for each volunteer and out of that they had to provide their own clothing.

February 16th Farmer Mr. Samson Blewitt of Pye Green was shot by poachers who were attempting to steal game from his farm. *The full incident is related in Anthony Hunt's book *Murder and Manslaughter around Cannock Chase.*

*Mr. Blewitt was also a night soil contractor (one who emptied toilet pits) for the gravel pit in High Town. Some 350 houses had been built in the Hednesford area since he had the contract.

March The Headline in the *Cannock Advertiser* was "A Periodic Complaint" and said,

> *"For over a week the dust has been almost intolerable in the streets of Hednesford town.*
> *This not only means a lot of extra work, but also considerable damage to goods. Would it*
> *not be possible for the Surveyor of the Urban District Council to order water carts to pay*
> *a visit to the town in the morning of each day, instead of in the afternoon."*

It would seem from this article that the main street of Hednesford town centre was still merely a dirt track or at least one of the few streets that had tarmac in the town and so dust from the others spread across the centre. As you will see later in the diary Hednesford's roads were only gradually being changed.

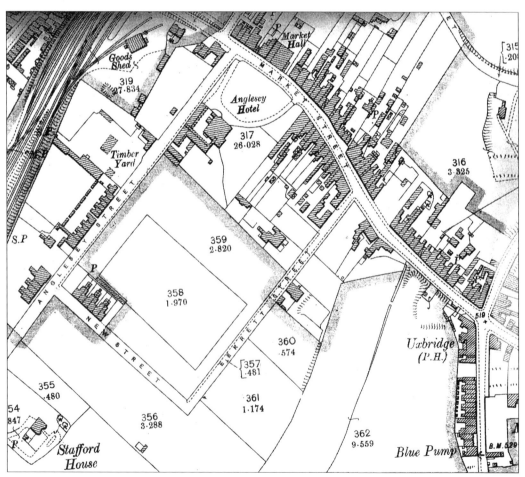

3. *Map of Market Street area 1902.*

4. Market Street, Hednesford 1904.

April The problem with roads continued, especially with the very narrow bridge into the town. Through mining in the area the road and pavement nearby had sunk some distance and the Council was asked to repair it for pedestrians. Their answer was to raise the fence on the Station Road approach to the bridge. ★The bridge problem would surface time and again.

April Queen Victoria's birthday celebrations – A procession through Hednesford saw men dressed in khaki and comical dress and they carried a coffin with the effigy of Kruger in it round "the Pool" and then on to the Anglesey lawn where a bonfire had been prepared. Several thousand were present entertained by a band supplied with whistles. When the bonfire was lit the figure, filled with fireworks, blazed away to the sound of crackers.

May A fire in a Market Street shop next to the Uxbridge Arms which was owned by Mr. Biningsley and sub let to Mr. Witts, the barber, began at 9.00 p.m. A lamp used to light the lock-up fell and set fire to the shop. Fortunately a fire hydrant was nearby, but by the time

5. Clarkes barber's shop next to the Uxbridge Arms.

3

the fire was put out damage had been done to the wooden structure, the walls and windows. Those small shops are still there today and one remained as a barber's for many years – Les Clark being the last men's barber there (see previous page).

★At the time Hednesford had no regular fire brigade, relying on that of Cannock to ride to its rescue. It would be some years, as you will read, before that was rectified.

May 19th On that Friday between 11 and 12 o'clock news reached Hednesford that Mafeking had been relieved. The bells at collieries rang out. The following morning a general holiday was declared and the streets became a mass of flags. In Wimblebury the White Star Band paraded the village.

6. Celebration for the relief of Mafeking in Ebenezer Street.

June 23rd A public meeting was held at the Drill Hall in Victoria Street to try to decide how the men who were fighting in the Boer War might be commemorated. Councillor Stanley said that monies raised at the present should be used to look after the families of those fighting, but was in favour of some sort of memorial. It was decided that the idea of erecting almshouses or baths should be dropped. Councillor Mason advocated the idea of obtaining ground which could be planted with trees and used for public recreation. Major Williamson suggested a small park and believed that the Marquis of Anglesey would supply the land. The most obvious place would be "the Pool" which had running water. He thought it might be laid out with a lake for boating in the summer and ice skating in the winter. He also thought if the local collieries were approached "a nice little sum" might be raised. A committee of eighteen was formed to look into the idea.

★*Historical note* – Hednesford Pool had gradually dried up after Bentley Brook was diverted to avoid flooding in Pool Pit (site of today's Museum of Cannock Chase) and by 1900 was just a marshy area, but only in winter. In the past the Pool had been used for fishing and duck shooting and when Thomas Eskrett had the Anglesey Hotel in the 1860's and 1870's he hired boats out and kept them in a small boathouse on the Pool.

June 28th Celebrations in Hednesford after the news of the fall of Pretoria, South Africa. The parade was timed to leave the Anglesey Grounds at six o'clock. Flags decorated the various streets and a very large crowd gathered at the Station Bridge and along Market Street. Many older residents said that they had not seen such a huge crowd since the Army Manoeuvres on the Chase in 1873. The procession which was over half a mile included a decorated motor car, sixty horsemen, volunteers, a naval squad and the band of Company F of the 2nd V.B. South Staffs. Definitely not PC today was "a representation of South African natives clothed in animal skins and armed with assegais".

Unfortunately with such a massive gathering accidents happened, especially at the corner of Station Bridge and Cannock Road. The cannon on the miniature man-of-war was fired and two or three people were struck by portions of the wad. One lady "who was very upset" was taken into the Beehive shop to recover.

December 29/30th The worst fire that Hednesford had experienced happened in the early hours of Sunday at Messrs. Ives and Westwood grocery and provisions store in Market Street, close to Victoria Street. Mr. Allen saw a blaze in the upper storey of the shop and he raised the alarm and a messenger was sent to the police station along Cannock Road. He then raced to Mr. Arnott's who promptly called for the fire brigade with the "steam bull" of West Cannock Colliery. About twenty minutes after the alarm was raised the hose and reel, which was kept at Mr. Mason's along Station Road, arrived, but with only one fireman, Mr. Martin. With the assistance of P.C. Cook they attached the hose to the hydrant outside Lloyd's Bank and fought the blaze.

Eventually another fireman arrived. The call was made to the Cannock Brigade at 5 o'clock and the "Edith May" arrived at Hednesford at 5.20 a.m. The fire was then confined to the upper floor, but the shop was considerably damaged.

1901

January Trooper W. Twigg returned home after being wounded. His father was the manager of East Cannock Colliery. A list if of the sick and injured appeared in March and included Volunteer J. Buckley who was laid up in the Transvaal with enteric fever.

April 18th The first general meeting of the Hednesford Traders Association was held at the Anglesey Hotel.

May A row of new houses was built at Rawnsley by the Cannock & Rugeley Colliery Company. Most of them are still there today just above the Trafalgar Inn.

7. 197/207 Littleworth Road c.1950.

8. 403/417 Littleworth Road c.1950.

May/July Some of the Volunteers arrived back from the Front in South Africa. However, news had not reached the people of Hednesford and Privates Powis, Perry, Seabury and Neville arrived to an almost empty railway station owing to an alteration in the train time. The Company men and Band did meet them and they were escorted to the Drill Hall. On the Thursday evening (May 23rd) they were given a dinner at the Anglesey Hotel. On July 26th Private Buckley, who had remained behind in South Africa due to illness, arrived home by the 8.30 p.m. train and was met by the Company and Band. Once again they went to the Anglesey for refreshments.

★The only Volunteer not to return from the war was Private John Edward Reynolds who died during military action.

June Mr. Melling, General Manager of West Cannock Colliery Company, died aged 42 from acute pneumonia at Stafford House. A local councillor representing a ward in Hednesford he originated in Leicestershire.

★Historical Note – Stafford House was built sometime in the mid-nineteenth century. The first owner for sure was Thomas Cliffe, horse trainer, who moved there in 1874 after a serious accident. He died in 1881 and not long after it was purchased by the West Cannock Colliery Company as a house for their manager, the first probably being Stephen H. Terry in 1890, a civil mechanical engineer at the pit. After Melling's death Charles Fisher (44), colliery manager, moved in with his family, followed by Mr. Smithurst. Archie Robert Latham moved there in 1928 and stayed until he retired in 1963 when he moved to Wales to keep a hotel. The house was then demolished to make way for a housing estate on the corner of Anglesey Street and Stafford Lane reaching down to Cornwall Drive.

The original boundary went down Stafford Lane to Ridings Brook in the dip. Almost all

the fields on that side belonged to Stafford House, including the cottage in the dip where the gardener for the house (Fred Drury) lived. On the opposite side of the lane were fields where Mr. Stanton kept his pigs (he used to make his own pork pies). Pat Collins usually held his fair on the rough ground (the junction of Eskrett Street and Cornwall Road).

9. John Latham outside Stafford House.

10. Stafford Lane with cottage 1920.

June Rawnsley School - A report by H.M. Inspector for Schools said of the Mixed Department of the school, "The accommodation at present is insufficient for the average attendance. This should at once be remedied or the grant next year will be endangered." The Council recommended that space be added to fit a further 90 pupils.

July Mr. Collins's Circus visited Hednesford and set up on the Anglesey Recreation Ground. Mr. Bird, a local barber and assistant to Mr. Maxted of Market Street, undertook to shave the lion tamer in the cage with Wallace, the male lion, still in there. A lioness was also in there and Mr. Bird "caused considerable amusement in the crowd by continually looking round to see where the lioness was".

September Mr. Tomkinson's Royal Gipsy Children performed at the Drill Hall. They did feats of equilibrium, juggling and trapeze. Locals also sang and told minstrel jokes.

1902

March Members of F Company of the 2nd V.B. Regiment had their annual supper at the Anglesey Hotel and afterwards adjourned to the Drill Hall for the unveiling of the memorial tablet to those eight men who went to South Africa. When the Drill Hall ceased to be the headquarters for the Volunteers the tablet was repositioned outside the Soldiers Club in Anglesey Street where it is today.

11. Boer War memorial tablet.

May 24th The first mention of the district possibly installing electricity for lighting for streets.

> "A provisional order to empower the Council to have electricity was obtained some time ago at considerable cost. The action was taken principally because a private company was intending to obtain similar powers. The Council was informed that within two years of the granting of the order by the Government it must light some portion of its district. Mr. Frank Broadbent, MIEC of London, friend of Councillor Mason, proposed electric light and destructor works to make it economically viable because the area was "not one that was most suitable for profitable electric lighting".

The Council had invested heavily in gas lighting and some Councillors were loathe to support the new venture. The total number of gas lamps in the whole area was 11,232. However, as time progressed it was decided to apply for the order by December, 1903. For the Hednesford area the council proposed to light the following:-

1. Wimblebury Road and areas around the railway.
2. Cross Keys and railway areas.
3. The road from Rawnsley to Cannock Wood along with railway areas.
4. The road from Hednesford to Hazel Slade along with railway areas.
5. In High Town – Burgoyne Street, Bradford Street, Queen Street and Platt Street.
6. Green Heath and Pye Green – Cross Street, Pye Green, Blewitt Street, Abbey Street, Heath Street, Top Abbey Street and Ebenezer Street.
7. In Hednesford – Market Street, the Bridge area, Rugeley Road including the Bridge area, High Mount and Mount Street, McGhie Street, Anglesey Street, Eskrett Street, Victoria Street, Prince Albert Street, Reservoir Road and streets, New Street, George Street and Pump Street.
8. Wimblebury – Piggott Street, Arthur Street, Glover Street and King Street.

★The railway companies were to be asked to share the costs in those areas where they had interests. Surprisingly wording in the order made specific mention that most of the above streets were "not repairable" by the Council, but the responsibility of the residents.

★Also notice the number of street names which no longer exist today.

June 13th Permanent Memorial of Peace for Hednesford – Members of the Hednesford Cycle Parade Committee met with locals at the Public Rooms with the idea of pursuing the suggestion of reviving the idea of "the Pool" as a park. It was decided a deputation of eight should ask the Cannock and Rugeley Colliery Company if they had any further thoughts on the matter of finance.

June 18th Coronation arrangements. The weekly meeting which took place at Church Hill School decided to accept the tender from the Anglesey Hotel to provide 300 hundred dinners at a cost of 1s 8d per head. Each person would receive a ticket, value 3d, for drinks. A tent on the Anglesey lawn would be erected for the elderly. A sum of 10s was to be allocated to convey the old people from Hazel Slade. The idea of a bonfire on Hednesford Hills was finally agreed upon after some heated discussion. (The South Staffordshire Waterworks Company gave permission to set up fireworks on the embankment of the reservoir.) All the children of the district would be presented with a Coronation mug (some 2,200 children at a cost of £27 10s). It was also decided to have sports activities to provide for those not included in other events.

The children were to assemble for tea at 3.30 p.m. on the Thursday and a dinner given to the elderly at one o'clock on the Friday. The Salvation Army Band would play on both days.

1903

January Mr. Wolverson, missionary to the Boatman's Hall, told the Council that there had been more than 500 visits by boatmen in 1902, with over 1,000 visits to the coffee room which was run by Mr. & Mrs. W. Lowe. 3,000 copies of "The Waterman" had been sold.

January The dangerous condition of the Hazel Slade Bridge was considered and a scheme to improve the arch at a cost of £90 was to be undertaken.

January The Council received a letter from the General Post Office which said there was no objection to changing the name of Five Ways to Heath Hayes.

April The New Connexion Church at High Town had a new organ installed.

May The Council agreed to the making of new streets in High Town – namely Bradford Street, Queen Street and Platt Street. The dirt tracks would disappear and tarmac introduced.

12. Provident House, High Town with Queen Street in the background.

August Proposal to build a workman's institute in Market Street (the New Club) consisting of a reading room, billiard room and assembly room for 500 people. It was not in any way officially associated with the Miners' Union, being an independent institution and for all workers. The opening of the Hednesford Progressive Club took place on Monday June 26th, 1905 at a cost of £2,000. At the first Annual Meeting it was announced that the rooms were being well used and the Club had over 1,000 members.

October Passive Resistance to the Education Act (1902)

The Education Act (1902) stated that School Boards were to be abolished and replaced by Local Education Authorities and the voluntary schools were to receive further financial aid out of the rates. The intention was to bring order to the system. However, there was considerable resistance from the non-conformists, for example Baptists and Methodists, who resented paying rates to support the schools where the Anglican Creed was taught. In July 1903 the Citizens League was formed to protest. Their action would be to withhold their payment of rates. Many were arrested and prosecuted and sent to jail.

On August 8th a meeting had been held at the Wesleyan Schoolroom to organise passive resistance to the Act. In Hednesford local Methodists in particular refused to pay the portion of rates destined for education. Rather than arrest them (some were local Councillors) the police were instructed to seize the protestors' goods and sell them in auction to make up the money. On Tuesday October 6th those goods came up for auction at the rear of Hednesford

Police Station. Mr. Lockett, the Auctioneer and a Non-Conformist himself, said that he was against what the Government was doing and he would act for free. All the goods were bought by Mr. R. Hughes and Mr. W. Gellion, members of the Citizens League. There was an attempt by outside bidders to buy goods, but the auctioneer ignored them. The League would then return the goods to the owners who donated the auction prices to the League. In all eighteen local men were involved, including Mr. Mason, Mr. Moore and Mr. Goscomb, respected businessmen in the town.

These sales of goods continued for the next four years until the Government finally passed a Bill to relieve the grievances in March, 1907.

1904

February Residents of Anglesey Street complained to the council about the "disgraceful condition" of the street. They intimated that the principal house holders were willing to pay for proper repairs. Remember the local authority had disclaimed any responsibility for street repairs. In June the Council agreed to do the work, but it would cost £442 5s 3d.

February 23rd On that Tuesday a water main burst along Rugeley Road. "The road was rendered quite impassable and what was once "the Pool" again became a sheet of water."

June At a previous Council meeting it was decided to kerb, channel and make Eskrett Street. A petition by owners of the street protested saying that "all necessary repairs had been done under the supervision of the Surveyor". They argued that "there was little traffic and the amount of property in the street was not sufficient to warrant the work being undertaken and it was not a public necessity". One difficulty was that a new house needed sewering and could not be drained into Anglesey Street. The Council overcame that by ruling that the matter should be dealt with by the owner. Eskrett Street improvements would remain in abeyance.

13. Hednesford from Hill Top c.1920.

July 1st On Friday afternoon a drayman was taking three barrels of liquor in a lorry up Market Street towards Church Hill when his horse suddenly started outside Mr. Maxted's shop. A hogshead of brandy was dislodged and fell into the street, breaking as it hit the kerb. The spirit flowed down the street and only a little was rescued by people who were quickly on the spot with cups or dishes. The brandy order was for Mr. W. Ormson, landlord of the Uxbridge Arms. The loss was over £60.

July The Council discussed the possible sites for an electric light station to light Cannock. They included at the rear of the Council offices; the bridges near "The Hills", a private house in Old Hednesford Road next to today's railway bridge and the council depot; brewery land near Cannock Railway Station; or the sewerage farm. For cost purposes the Council office site was preferred. It also discussed Hednesford saying that "provision should be made for electric light to be taken to Hednesford" believing, so the engineer advised, that Hednesford would pay.

October 2nd About one o'clock on Sunday afternoon Mr. Tong of the Star Tea Company was walking along Market Street when he noticed flames in the front shop of Messrs. Moore and Company Clothing Factory. He raised the alarm and the shop was quickly opened and the flames attacked. Messrs. Tong, Simcox, Stanton and Moore, along with other neighbours helped to carry water to the fire. A small hose was attached to the water pipe and helped to reduce the fire. Mr. Martin brought the cart and hose from the Police Station. The fire was soon under control and the majority of the stock saved. The Fire Brigade from Cannock arrived promptly, but were not needed.

November A deputation to the Council of Hednesford Traders concerning the fire appliances at Hednesford suggested the following improvements:-

1. Another hydrant be placed halfway between the Anglesey Hotel and the Uxbridge Arms.
2. A printed notice on the shed door which contained the hose cart, giving information on where the key was to be found on breaking the glass.
3. A horse cart to be provided because of the hilly nature of the area and the weight to be carried.
4. A list of hydrants and firemen with their addresses put up in the Police Station.
5. A key of the hose shed to be labelled and attached to the notice.
6. Plates put up notifying the position of the hydrants.
7. A new fire escape to be purchased for Hednesford and a standard provided.

★Remember the performance they had had with the fire in Market Street?

1905

January The gas lights in Market Street failed. Just before 11.00 p.m. the gas lights in the houses and the street lamps went out because the one gas holder of the two had become exhausted before the person in charged was aware of it and switched to the other. As soon as his own lights dimmed he ran to switch on the full holder. The incident only lasted two minutes. The same had happened five years before. It could have proved dangerous had people gone to bed leaving the gas on.

November The Council agreed to go ahead with electric street lighting. The cost would be £3,000 for a part experiment in certain areas. They hoped to persuade the gas company to service more houses. The Hednesford Traders Association objected if all ratepayers had to pay towards the cost saying, "That this meeting protests in the strongest possible manner against the expenditure of ratepayers' money as an experiment either in Cannock or Hednesford having had such conclusive evidence of the complete failure of electric supply in other such compact towns."

1906

February Father O'Keefe acquired Mount Pleasant for the Catholic Church which was tenanted by Mr. G. Lunt with rooms reserved for Father O' Keefe. A resident priest for Hednesford was then a possibility.

March The Shropshire, Worcestershire and Staffordshire Electric Supply Company would take over the order to supply it. It was hoped that "within 20 months it would supply the centre of Hednesford and 500 yards along Station Road".

April 6th A fire broke out at Mr. Green's house in Abbey Street, Green Heath. He had left a lighted lamp in the stable and it was possibly kicked over by his horse. It was discovered at 8 o'clock, by which time the stable was in flames with the horse tethered inside. It managed to break free, but was badly burnt. Police and neighbours put the fire out. However, panic had ensued at the start as the alarm bell could not be rung loudly as the rope broke. P.C. Hodson had to climb on the roof to hand ring it.

On the Sunday evening, April 7th, there was a fire on Hednesford Hills, but no culprits were found.

August 10th The Council approved the new contract with the Cannock, Hednesford and District Gas Company for the gas lighting of Hednesford with instructions to fix incandescent lamps in Market Street.

September 2nd The common on Hednesford Hills was set alight on the Sunday by four youths. It resulted in damage to an acre and a half of heather and gorse as well as some

14. West Hill, Hednesford c.1920 with Albert Stanley's house on the right.

property of the Cannock and Rugeley Colliery Company. The lads were caught and at Penkridge Police Court they were found guilty. Oswell Birch of Blakemore Street was fined 40s as the main offender; Noah Slade of Littleworth, 20s; and Jos. Wilkes of Littleworth and William Slack of Reservoir Road were each fined 10s.

★Fires on Hednesford Hills are still a problem today!

November A new Fire Station was proposed for Hednesford. Possible sites included the old gas works; land adjoining Dr. Edmundson's at the gravel hole; a field opposite West Cannock's No. 3 Pit; or West Hill.

The West Hill site was preferred as it had a covered in yard on the premises belonging to Mr. Albert Stanley. He would lease it out for 7 years with an annual rent of £35 with an option to purchase it for £450 to take immediate effect.

1907

March Eremon, trained by Tom Coulthwaite won the Grand National, the second winner from our area. In 1910 he repeated the feat with Jenkinstown winning and in 1931 he won again with Grakle, becoming the first trainer to win three Grand nationals. ★More details in *Hednesford's Horse Racing History* by your author.

July Finally Hednesford was to get its own Fire Station. The house would be leased from Mr. Albert Stanley on West Hill for £19 10s per annum with the Council paying the rates. The present manure pit and wall was to be removed from the front entrance to the site and a new pair of doors with glazed panels to be fitted. The ceiling of the house was to be matchboard, the floor levelled to that of the yard and the station to be paved with blue dust bricks. A partition wall was to be raised and shelving provided.

Street making – Anglesey Street had already been made and now the Council considered Bradford Street and Queen Street at High Town as well as McGhie Street in Hednesford. Councillor Mason argued that McGhie Street should take preference as "part of it was dangerous and as it had been opened at the top end for traffic (High Mount Street) it should be done first". He also stated that "so much more work has been done at Chadsmoor than at Hednesford".

December There was a meeting at the Drill Hall about the possibility of opening a Co-op Store in Hednesford.

Historical note – The Cooperative Movement began in Rochdale in 1844 and included distributing a share of its profits, "the divi". In 1862 it gained legal status and by 1863 the Cooperative Society began. In 1873 it was involved in importing, ship owning and overseas ventures. By 1900 it had a total of 1435 registered shops and in 1942 it opened its first self-service shop in London. 90% of all self-service shops were operated by the Coop in 1950.

1908

January Messrs. Moore & Company entertained over 300 employees and friends at a Christmas Party at the Drill Hall. Mr. Higgins, foreman of the making up department, said, "A certain amount of pride in their work had seen a steady growth of the business from a comparatively small trade to its present dimensions."

Historical note – On May 11th, 1876 W.H. Moore had signed an underlease with Thomas Eskrett of the Anglesey Hotel to rent out plots 71, 73 and 75 next to the hotel and build his clothing factory in Hednesford, having left J. Shannon and Son Limited of Walsall. The factory occupied the site of today's Light Works and was one of the few employers of women in Hednesford. In the 1881 Census his family seem to be living on the premises, but by the late 1890's he occupied 113 Green Heath Road with his son, Ralph, living at No. 63, a house known locally as "Moore's Mansion" because of its many rooms and large gardens. W.H. Moore died in 1919, but Ralph continued the business. By the 1930's a Walsall company had taken it over, but in the early 1940's it closed down mainly because the firm lost the Government contract to make Army uniforms as they were proving too expensive. The Government wanted quantity not quality. The contract went to the Walsall side of the business. Parts of the old stables of the Anglesey Hotel were used to make clothing after that, but it soon closed. The factory was eventually taken over by Joseph Lucas Company

15. William Henry Moore.

in 1951 and assembled electric parts for cars e.g. blue flashing lamp for police cars.

★A DVD, **The Light Works,** telling the story of the factory is on sale at the Museum of Cannock Chase.

February 22nd Terrible gales hit the area causing lots of damage in Hednesford. A portion of fencing at Station Road School was blown away. West Hill Infants School had its roof damaged and tiles were blown off. The Boys School had the roof of one classroom blown off and a fallen chimney and the fence in front of the building blown away. At Littleworth a 12 house row had nearly all its windows blown out whist at the Castle Inn, tenanted by Mr. J. Gore, the chimney stack crashed through the roof. In Rawnsley one garden shed was carried several hundred yards before being smashed. In Market Street a large portion of corrugated iron hit shops on the opposite side of street to the Post Office, but little damage was caused. Finally at Green Heath a portion of the gable end of a house opposite the West Cannock Pit and near to the Fox Inn (house next to corner of Ebenezer Street) was blown out and the room exposed to the elements.

June The Council finally decided to number the houses in the area at a cost of £43 19s 2d. 5,135 houses had to be allocated a number. The postmen must have cheered! Contrary to some rumours No. 13 was used.

1909

February 2nd The Council approved the building of 3 more houses in Heath Street and 26 in High Mount Street.

Victoria Street – The Council were told of the poor state of the road. It was often used at night because of the Drill Hall as the only place for public meetings yet water was frequently allowed to stand in pools. Mr. Webster and Mr. Mason said that it had been used by the public for over twenty years and the Council ought to take it over. Some councillors thought the property owners should make it over first, but Mr. Webster objected as the public had destroyed what was once a private road. The decision was made that if the owners asked the Council to take over the street then they would see to its improvement.

May 15th Kier Hardy visited Hednesford to speak at the Drill Hall.

August 9th A fire at Isaiah Howells's china and hardware shop in Market Street broke

16. Hednesford scenes c.1920.

out on Monday night. Some children playing in Victoria Street noticed smoke coming from a long shed at the rear of the shop. The alarm was given and tradesmen fought the fire. They included four locals known a few years before as "The Auxiliary Fire Brigade". The hose and handcart was got from Mr. Hendry's and fixed to the hydrant opposite the Anglesey. Later the Fire Brigade from Cannock arrived and within an hour of their arrival the fire was extinguished.

When the alarm was first raised Mrs. Howells ran out to help, but the excitement caused her to be ill. On being taken into the house she collapsed and died just a little while later, despite help from Dr. Phillips.

October After the tragedy of Mrs. Howells the Council had a lengthy meeting to discuss improvements. Mr. Kent, Captain of the Fire Brigade, said that his sub-captain at Hednesford had frequently found a motor car, two or three bicycles and a lot of old harness in the place where the equipment was kept. The hose had been used by inexperienced people and after a fire at Stafford House a length of hose was found with several holes in it. As for the recent fire at Howells's store the firemen were not called out and knew nothing of the blaze until the fire was out. When they did arrive they were booed by some of the crowd. Asked if the Auxiliary Brigade should continue he said they should, but should be given "a few drills" and work closely with the actual Fire Brigade.

It was decided to keep the Auxiliary Brigade, but employ a further four firemen taking the number to twenty. Cards should also be displayed in Hednesford to enhance the communications in the event of another fire.

November 18th Mr. Barton applied to build a skating rink at Hednesford in Anglesey Street (the site of today's Co-op).

Optimism and Pessimism
(1910 - 1919)

Man will always look to the future for better things to come. Hednesford continued to grow and problems of the last decade were still met with enthusiasm, safe in the knowledge that they could be ironed out. Thank heavens no one could foresee what was on the horizon.

1910

January 12th After two months of construction Hednesford's Skating Rink was officially declared open, the ceremony being performed by the Marquis of Anglesey. The building was 100 feet by 50 feet and had the best quality maple floor equal to any in the Midlands. It had cloak rooms, lavatories, a cycle store and a modern system of heating. Special provision had also been made for spectators and non roller skaters.

In his speech Mr. McLaren said, "The building of the Rink marked a very distinct step for Hednesford which had long ago passed the line which divided a village from a town. The opening of the Progressive Club and the Rink were events which stood out as milestones on the road of progress from a town to a city." (Cheers and Laughter) Reverend Quibell added, somewhat humorously, that when Hednesford became a city St Peter's would naturally become a cathedral and he a bishop. Optimism indeed!

On **March 10th** the first Skating Carnival was held with over 60 skaters in fancy dress.

17. Skating Rink/Electric Palace c.1920, opposite the Anglesey.

February The Council were urged to attend to "the shocking state of High Mount Street (a new street, but still a dirt track). Reverend Pimblett said, "It had already been the death of one poor horse that could not pull through the horrible mire which was a scandal to the neighbourhood and a disgrace to civilisation."

March Dr. J.N. Phillips urged the Council to deal with the state of Eskrett Street "to make it a proper sanitary street instead of the filthy by-way which it was". The Council would consider the sewering of the street although they had been petitioned not to make, curb or channel it by some residents. Dr. Phillips's house and surgery was along that street.

March Jenkinstown, trained by Tom Couthwaite, won the Grand National, the third winner in our area. More details found in *Hednesford's Horse Racing History* by your author.

May Memorial services were held in the area for Edward VII.

There was a possibility of airship trials over Hednesford Hills. Mr. Brough, a friend of Mr. Shepherd, a motor engineer, was trying to arrange them.

August 21st, Rawnsley's 24th Annual Flower Show took place with a pit pony show, horse leaping, many sports, including tug-of-war, cycle racing and much more.

1911

June Coronation Arrangements for Hednesford, including Littleworth, Hazel Slade and Chadsmoor. It was estimated that some 3,731 children would have to be served tea on the Thursday at the various schools. (Hednesford 1,150; Chadsmoor 1,430; Church Hill 388; St. Joseph's, Hill Top 135; Wimblebury 213; Rawnsley and Hazel Slade 415.) Following their tea the children from West Hill School, headed by the Boy Scouts Band, would be escorted to the Anglesey Field where sports would take place.

On the Friday the invitation dinner for the elderly would take place in a marquee on the Anglesey lawn at 4 o'clock. After their meal they would be taken to the Rink where Mr. Barton would give a show of cinematograph pictures and other entertainment. At dusk a firework display would take place. Similar events would take place at the other venues. Each area would present the children with a commemorative item to record the event.

July Bradbury Lane Wesleyan Mission - On Monday July 3rd Mrs. J. Smithurst, accompanied by her husband, Councillor Smithurst, laid the foundation stone for two new class or vestry rooms, the land being provided by West Cannock Colliery Company. The stone, which can still be seen today, bears the inscription "To the Glory of God. This stone was laid by Mrs. Smithurst of Stafford House, Hednesford on behalf of the friends and members of the Mission July 3rd, 1911."

August Pye Green water supply – Because of its geographical position the village had to rely on wells for its water, 16 in all. However, of those only 9 were safe for public use with 4 suspicious and 3 unsafe. Dr. Phillips, as one of the Council Medical Officers, told them that it would be a "general boon to the inhabitants of Pye Green if the South Staffs Water Company could possibly supply it". The Council agreed to do everything it could to persuade the water company to supply.

18. Memorial Stone at Bradbury Lane Mission.

17

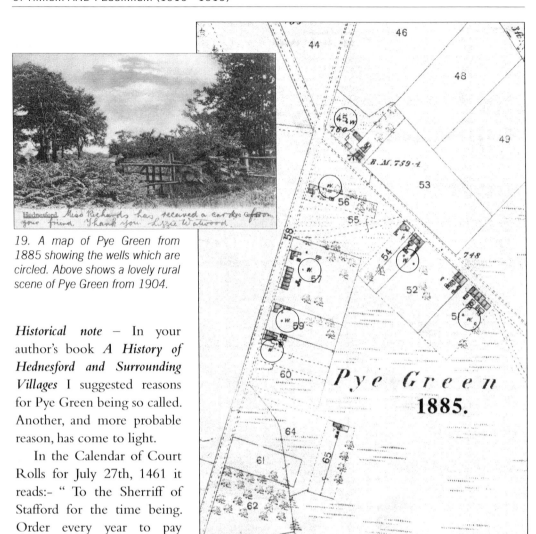

19. A map of Pye Green from 1885 showing the wells which are circled. Above shows a lovely rural scene of Pye Green from 1904.

Historical note – In your author's book *A History of Hednesford and Surrounding Villages* I suggested reasons for Pye Green being so called. Another, and more probable reason, has come to light.

In the Calendar of Court Rolls for July 27th, 1461 it reads:- " To the Sherriff of Stafford for the time being. Order every year to pay Roger Pye, late Yeoman of the Chamber of Richard, Duke of York, 6d a day during his life as for the good and praiseworthy service to himself (Richard) and to his said father. The King (Henry VI) has granted to him for life the office of Ranger of the Forest of Canke to be occupied by himself or deputy, taking of the issues, profits, farms and revenues of the said County, the fees, wages and profits to that office due and accustomed in the time of King Edward III or Richard II."

James Pye was the last of the family to inherit that title in the seventeenth century and thoughts are that he lived near today's water tower.

October 11th The Empire Cinema opened with Mr. F.M. Barker as proprietor. In **October, 1912** it was refurbished with 600 seats downstairs and 200 in the balcony.

November Mr. Roland Barton wanted to launch "The Hednesford Cooperative Electric Palace Company" to enable the Rink to show moving pictures. It would cost £3,000 and shares could be bought for 10 shillings each. It was obviously successful as in **May 1912** the building had become a partial cinema with "animated pictures" being shown regularly on Saturdays and Mondays while skating continued on the remainder of the nights. On Fridays he even held dances.

December 14th Fire broke out at the Old Hednesford Colliery, Hill Street, killing five men. More of this episode in *A History of Hednesford and Surrounding Villages* by your author.

1912

January The Gas Purchase Question – The Council met to decide whether or not to purchase the local gas works and company which still fed most homes and some streets with lighting. In a recent poll of residents 881 were in favour and 1108 against. It was decided to leave matters as they were.

February/March A Miners Strike hit the local pits.

February 10th On the Saturday evening a fire broke out in Holland's Cinematographic Theatre on the Anglesey Field. It began in the centre of the roof which was made of tarpaulin and within half an hour had destroyed the whole roof. A large crowd gathered, but the police did excellent work in controlling them. Mr. Barton lent a fire extinguisher which saved the organ. Disaster was averted by the police who forced three men from the roof who were trying to save part of it by cutting away the burning canvas. Mr. Arthur Holland said that the fire was probably started by a spark from the traction engine which stood alongside the tent, though coke fires inside could have been to blame.

February/June Moore's Factory Strike began when Mr. Moore wanted to change workers' pay for particular jobs in the machine room. They insisted it would mean a cut in wages and about 100 machinists refused to work with the new pay structure.

20. Moore's "Angels".

The argument really began when the Trades Board had agreed to pay rises for the industry. Moore's argument was that large factories in cities could afford the rises, but his small business could not. His idea was to raise the lower paid labour a step or two until it reached the Trades Board level. The local Cannock Miners Union representative stepped in to help the girls, but Moore refused to deal with him until the girls had joined a union. Arrangements were made to picket the Works.

July The Government had passed the Closing Order Bill which was a step towards regulating closing hours for shops. Beforehand shops could choose their own hours. (You could get a haircut at almost midnight in Victorian Hednesford).

December In response to the opening of The Empire Mr. Barton applied for a license to hold Sunday Concerts at the Electric Palace. ★Sunday was still regarded as a day of rest where nothing but church should happen and certainly not business. This question would crop up time and again.

His first application was refused, but when it was pointed out that The Empire had been granted one for an event Mr. Mason argued that, although the Council did not want it to grow into a business, they ought to be consistent in their decisions. The license was then granted.

1913

February Pye Green Sewerage – The village was still without a sewerage system and when the Council discussed the matter one councillor asked, "Is it wise to build sewers when coal mining could cause their collapse?" 12 houses had been built on the Pye Green Road with water closets, but excreta was running out on to local land. The matter would be held in abeyance, but in the September it was getting worse with sewerage being deposited on local land opposite. Councillor Earnest Lindop declared that the "stench was abominable" and added, "Are we living in the twentieth century?"

April Some years previously traders had been allowed to "dress out" their shops (put goods on the pavement), but it had become a problem for pedestrians. The Council now wanted the practice to be abolished. There was also the question of too many vacant houses in the area. Mr. Mason said that he remembered the time twenty years before when council houses were at £7 10s and the boom time when labourers could get 6d per hour, but with the slump miners left the district and houses stood empty. Should more houses be built?

April 12th Stafford Lane, Hednesford was the scene of a remarkable accident. For some weeks about forty men employed by the London and North Western Railway Company had been demolishing the bridge near High Town. The top courses of the arch had been removed when suddenly the arch collapsed, plummeting men, barrows and tools down 25 foot. Six men were injured, but fortunately no bones broken. Doctors Phillips and Waddell examined the men at the scene before sending them home to Walsall.

June Hednesford Traders objected to the Council's refuse tip on Hednesford Hills, adjacent to the Rugeley Road as it was "an eyesore and detrimental to health". In August 1915 the Council agreed to level the tip and grass it over.

By **August** Cannock Chase Coal Owners Rescue Station had opened in Victoria Street. *Historical note* – Cannock, Hednesford and District Gas Company had stopped production of gas at Hednesford and the disused buildings and land were sub-let by the Marquis of Anglesey to the local mining companies as a base for their rescue station. The lease, dated October 19th, 1912 stated "All that plot or parcel of land forming the north corner of the premises fronting Victoria Street, together with the buildings thereon" were sub-let. After training Joshua Payton became the first superintendent and his two sons, Ernest and Albert assistant superintendent and instructor respectively.

★As you can imagine people in the area had a little more to worry about during the following four years and the newspapers reflected that by concentrating on "news from the Front". But life must go on and the mundane aspects of life continued, though with less reporting.

21. Cannock Chase Miners Rescue Team.

1914

February The Council decided that street lighting by gas lamp should be reduced at night, but would possibly have new ones at the Uxbridge Corner and near the bridge down East Cannock Road.

July Hednesford Traders outing to Bridgnorth, Shropshire. They went in motor cars and while there visited the castle and had boat trips down the Severn.

22. Hednesford Traders outing to Bridgnorth.

August The Great War – The Hednesford Company of Territorials left Hednesford on Sunday 2nd for their annual training at St. Asaph led by Captain Burnett and Lieutenants Ivatt and Green, but because of the seriousness of the situation they had returned by Monday at 8.30 pm. to await orders. They marched to the Drill Hall from the station and were dismissed, but 120 of the 125 stayed at the camp instead of going home. The order for mobilisation came at 8.00 p.m. on the Tuesday, but they were not to move out until the next morning. Many wives, sisters and sweethearts remained in the vicinity of the Drill Hall. On the Wednesday morning, with pay books distributed, they began their nine mile march to headquarters in Walsall.

Reverend Quibell addressed them before they set out finishing with, "I bid you God speed and hope that the good Lord may go with you and that you will return home safely in the end." The men were cheerful and as they stepped along Victoria Street they sang the refrain "When I am 21." Only today do we know the poignancy of that song.

23. Reverend Quibell with parishioners c.1910.

★Hednesford had the honour of sending the strongest Company in the 5th Battalion of the South Staffordshire Regiment. 50 army or navy reservists from Hednesford also received their orders to go to war, making them the largest contingent from the district.

★All three officers mentioned in the above died during the war.

October The Belgian Refugees – On Monday October 26th at 3.45 p.m. a group of 25 refugees, along with the 32 who were to live at Cannock, arrived at Hednesford Station and were greeted by huge crowds. Accommodation had been arranged for them at the Rescue Station and Gas Works in Victoria Street and local people had equipped the rooms out for their comfort. Mr. R. Jones provided his charabanc to take them from the station to the Drill Hall where a reception had been prepared. Various speeches welcomed them and the sacrifice their country had made in the War was spoken of and it was hoped that the men would soon find work in the area and be happy with their stay.

December Despite the War (which everyone had predicted would be over by Christmas) the Hednesford Traders went ahead with the town's Christmas celebrations. At least it might take their minds off what was happening elsewhere. Various shops went out of their way to make their displays better than usual.

They included – Allen Bros., pork butchers; Ball & Rigby, outfitters; "The Busy Bee", clothiers and fancy goods; Foster Bros., clothiers; Edwards, fruiterers; Whittle, pharmacist; and the Bon Marche, all of Market Street; as well as Benton & Charles, plumbers and decorators; T.H. Brown, clothiers and furniture; Marston, shoes and boots; Mellors, tobacconist; and Wighams of the "Bee Hive", all on Station Road or Cannock Road. In McGhie Street was W. Richards, ale and spirits, while Cannock Chase Motor Company of Uxbridge Street also took part. Finally, Messrs. T. Evans & Company, run by Mr. Ernest Lindop, coal agents for the Midlands and builders merchants, were also represented.

★By the end of the year West Cannock Colliery Company had started to sink the downcast shaft on their newest colliery, No. 5. By 1916 they had completed the upcast shaft. Bounded by Brindley Heath Road and Rugeley Road it was the last mine sunk in the Hednesford area. Originally access was from the Brindley Heath Road, but eventually Walker's Rise Bridge was built over the railway line to allow access from Rugeley Road.

24. West Cannock No. 5 Pit.

1915

January A dispute broke out between the contractors and carpenters who were working on the Military Camp on the Chase. The constructors had promised "overtime, good wages and sleeping accommodations on site", the wages being ten and a half pence per hour for carpenters and six and a half pence for labourers.

On arriving on site they found themselves three and a half miles from the site and no accommodation. They began work on the distinct understanding that all time would be paid, including getting to the site, and work at all times, even in wet weather. What they actually found was no pay if it rained and the six pence per day allowed for walking to the site would be stopped. Because of that they went on strike. The dispute was eventually settled and by March up to 500 huts had been practically completed. The work on the isolation hospital was complete and the extension to Brocton Camp well on its way with over a mile of additional line having been laid.

The training camp finally opened in May.

March/May The Belgian Refugees – In March a letter from "One Who Knows" stated, "I believe we have about eighteen Belgians stationed at Hednesford living under conditions which are not of a very high standard." It went on to say that the refugees were all sleeping in one room and only had one room to sit in at night. The writer complained of the lack of meals provided and the facilities. One Belgian he quoted paid £1 per week for his board (more than the average Englishman), but was under the following restrictions – He had to be indoors by 9.30 or 10.00 p.m. or be locked out; he must mend his own clothes; must not stay away from work if he is fit to go; and his meals are 8.30 breakfast at work, 1 o'clock dinner at work and tea at 6 o'clock. No supper is provided. The letter finished by saying, "If the authorities cannot alter these conditions then the best way to remedy it is to advertise for homes and they can then get them off their hands."

As would be expected that letter brought several responses, the best coming from the Belgians themselves. A reporter from the *Cannock Advertiser* visited their home and was impressed with the living conditions provided by Mr. Jos. Payton. The fourteen men were "all right here; we quite content". As for rules while living there the Belgians had made them themselves. They were all at work and in the evening preferred to remain in their little "snug". As far as meals were concerned they were more than satisfied. Before leaving for work they had coffee, with breakfast and dinner supplied at work. All the men, apart from two, finished work at six o'clock. The two returned at 3.00 p.m. and had a light meal. They

25. *Belgian Refugees at Cannock Workhouse with Father O'Keefe and Mr. and Mrs. Spires, Master and Matron.*

laid the table for the others and then all fourteen sat down together for tea. 50% of their wage was paid to the Council, averaging 12s 3d per week; the remainder with all overtime was banked by the men to save until they returned home after the War. As for going into lodgings they would hate it as none of them spoke English. It must also be noted that nearly all the men came from Bruges and four of them were brothers.

The Belgians also managed to write a letter themselves pointing out mistakes in the complaint. 1. They have four meals a day. 2. The two men who work at the pit finish early and get an extra meal. 3. The room where they sleep is much too big for 14 men and could easily fit 30. 4. The dining room and the room where they smoke are also big. When they arrived at Hednesford there were 21 men, but 7 have gone elsewhere. The letter was signed by all the men – Oorlynck, De Smedt, Floers, Gevsert, Christiaens (the four brothers), Blomdell, Van den Broncke, Van den Berghe, Verschoore, Van den Bussche and Van Parys.

In May the Belgians presented Mr. Payton and his wife with an illuminated address for his work in making them comfortable while staying at the Mines Rescue Station.

October 9th The new schools at High Town should not be opened until May 1st, 1916 and the buildings should be offered to the military to use as a hospital. Mr. Mason asked if the West Cannock Colliery Company should be asked to light the schools with electricity. Mr Smithurst said the Company was already lighting up the military camp "which was bigger than Hednesford" and so the Council should ask them. The two councillors were told that the schools already had gas fittings and alterations would be needed.

November 16th Mr. Bumstead handed over his building in Anglesey Street, on the same side of the street as the Anglesey Hotel, for the use of the troops stationed in the area for their relaxation. The building had been built originally by Mr. Bumstead as an institute for young men to keep them out of public houses. Alterations at a cost of £225 had been carried out and it contained billiard, reading and writing rooms and a spacious tea room with a boiler system which provided constant hot water. In his opening address Col. Williamson said it would "provide those (troops) with a place where they could come and rest and enjoy some form of social intercourse, a place where there would be no temptation (alcohol)".

The building would be handed over to a Soldier's Committee, together with a caretaker's house and bowling green. (Mr. Bumstead had been generous to troops previously – in 1895 he had given £100 towards the building of the Drill Hall.) Success seemed to be on the way as between 300 and 400 troops had used the building the previous weekend.

As the War progressed its effects were beginning to be felt on the Home Front, something not previously experienced. Hednesford was no exception.

1916

February Shoppers were to be persuaded to shop during the day to avoid night time lights (Zeppelins had already attacked Staffordshire). The suggestion was that shops would close at 6.30 p.m. Monday, Tuesday, Wednesday and Friday (Thursday was a half day closing) and 9.00 p.m. on Saturday. Hednesford Traders wanted 7.00 p.m. in the week, suggested by Mr. Hewitt, while Mr. Brown advocated things remain as they were until further police notice. In **December** the Government had to say that they had not ordered "total extinction of lights at night" as had been ordered by many authorities in the Midlands, but had suggested that "lights should be restricted and those which were on should be shaded and efficient arrangements made so that they could be quickly put out in emergency".

26. Market Street c.1910.

Local businesses were beginning to feel the effects as many men had joined up, leaving them understaffed. West Cannock Colliery had seen 500 to 600 men enlist and other collieries had similar figures. For the first time in its history England saw tribunal courts set up to judge whether or not citizens should be forced to enlist. In **March** at Hednesford Mr. Mason, local builder, appealed that three of his men should be exempted. He usually employed between 60 and 70 men but was already down to just 10. They were exempted for three months, but had to drill with the V.T.C. Messrs. Bumstead and Chandler also appealed on behalf of one worker whom they lent out to help local farmers plough. Their firm had been asked by the Staffordshire Agricultural Committee. Result – three months exemption and drill with the V.T.C. There were many other cases in the area.

In **April** the *Cannock Advertiser* was forced to reduce its newspaper from 8 pages to 4. By December the Government had introduced "meatless days" and proposed "to make further orders prohibiting, both in places of public eating and private houses, the consumption of meat on certain days, namely meat, poultry and game". Hednesford responded accordingly, although it meant serious trade restrictions for some businesses.

★Interesting to note that for the first time in the area Cannock Urban Tribunal heard a case from a conscientious objector. Exemption was refused and the appellant was placed at the disposal of the military authorities for national work e.g. agriculture, mining or transport.

June Trustees of the late Mr. William Field sold the Littleworth Tileries to Mr. T.C. Longstaff of Hednesford and he would continue the works as from June 17th, 1916.

July 29th On a brighter note a successful Military Sports Day was held in the grounds of Stafford House, kindly lent by Mr. Smithurst. The proceeds would go to the funds of the Soldiers Club in Station Road where they had already provided thousands of teas to troops. The event was to further promote relations between Hednesford and the troops stationed nearby. A large crowd watched troops from the regiments at Penkridge Bank compete against locals in events like six-a-side football, the 100 yards flat race, the mile race, high jump and the tug-of war. Unusual events like grenade throwing and hat trimming also took place.

September 9th Mr. John Williamson died and was buried at Cannock Cemetery on Tuesday 12th, aged ninety two. He was born in June 1824 at Benton in Durham. At the age of eleven the family moved to Belmont Colliery where his father was a sinker and later to Shincliffe where John worked as a pit boy. In 1845, after studying mining engineering and in particular flooding prevention he moved to Trubshaw Colliery, North Staffordshire and in 1851 to West Hallam where he sank two shafts. 1865 saw him at Coppy Hall Colliery, Aldridge and while there he was appointed manager of the Cannock and Rugeley Colliery Company in 1868. His expertise was soon evident when he managed the sinking of Pool Pit, Hednesford, passing through water filled gravel beds.

He had also patented a device for lubricating coal tubs in 1863 and in 1877 devised a new safety lamp. He remained general manager of the Cannock and Rugeley Company until 1900 though he still remained as a consulting engineer. With his help more and more mines were opened and Hednesford grew considerably in size. "If success had not been achieved there would be no Hednesford," he often declared. The growth of Hednesford certainly was allied to his success in opening up the mining area and his Company were responsible for building many homes. So far as Cannock Wood was concerned he formed the Hazel Slade Land and Building Company and what was previously a swamp at Hazel Slade was drained and hundreds of miners' homes erected. His family lived in Cannock Wood House, but in 1903 it burnt down. It was rebuilt and named The Grange which still stands today as a residential home.

He became a member of the Local Board (forerunner to the Council) and in later life a J.P. He boasted that he once met George Stevenson while at his grandfather's and Robert Stevenson worked with his grandfather. Colonel R.S. Williamson, his son, was given those initials as a reminder of that meeting.

1917

January The Council discussed a scheme to turn more local land over to agriculture for the war effort. Allotments in Ebenezer Street were looked at. Mr. Mason said that "there was considerable common land at Brindley Heath and on the fringe of the adjoining common which had already been brought into cultivation and much good produce had been obtained". Even Hednesford Hills was looked at, but obviously proved too barren for agriculture as did "the Pool" area.

July The second Military Sports took place and about 200 soldiers from the Military Hospital attended. Mr. Smithurst once again lent out the grounds at Stafford House.

John Smithurst – He was born in South Wingfield, Derbyshire an ancient village where Mary Queen of Scots was once imprisoned. For 16 years his father, also John, was a member of the local School Board and John succeeded him. His first job was in the Blackwell Colliery and later he was a deputy in Stanton Ironworks. After that he was under-manager for six years at a pit in the South Leicestershire Colliery and for two years a manager at South Wingfield Colliery. Around twenty years ago he had come to Hednesford as a certified manager at the West Cannock Collieries and after serving in that capacity for ten years he became agent and manager of the collieries.

He was first elected to the Council on May 31st, 1911 to represent Hednesford and was chairman for a year (1918/19). He was also president of the Ancient Order of Shepherds, the largest friendly society in the district with over a thousand members, and treasurer of the Station Road Soldiers Club.

1918

May A four hour storm of torrential rain and lightning hit the area causing damage. Water rushed through houses in Hednesford in the low lying streets. At Church Hill and West Hill a good deal of damage was done to the roadways, the exceptional volume of water washing away all building material and scattering loose stones and bricks everywhere. Many roads were flooded and debris washed down Church Hill and West Hill and into the town itself.

June Hednesford Railway Bridge was becoming a growing problem due to its very narrow footpath by the railway station. Suggestions for improvement included widening the footpaths. It was also suggested that the Council should pay for the repairs and then they would have far more control over the condition of the bridge. However, they decided to ask the railway company to make the bridge better.

27. Railway along the Rugeley Road c.1905.

November Influenza outbreak – Dr. Clendinnen, Medical Officer for Health, said that the new epidemic had "all the symptoms of the old disease, but it was more fatal". He stated that he did not believe that it was swine fever due to the poor quality of food, nor was it due to the lowered vitality of the people because of the lack of nutrition as the troops in France who were exceedingly well fed had fallen victim to the disease as much as the civilian population. On November 2nd he advised all elementary schools to close, the same with Sunday Schools. On November 9th he advised that picture palaces should also close as well as public houses, chapels and churches.

Local schools had reopened after three weeks, but some 1,500, a quarter of those on the books, had been absent. In Wimblebury the figure was as low as 50% attendance. In December he reported that the death rate in the area was 57 out of every thousand (128 deaths). The heaviest period for deaths was from November 8th to the 18th when the deaths totalled 69. In all Cannock had 14, Bridgtown 9, Hednesford 21, Littleworth 15, Chadsmoor 30 and Heath Hayes 16. Owing to the number of deaths the local undertakers had considerable delays in burials and the colliery companies helped in making coffins.

1919

January New council cemetery for Hednesford – Proposals were put forward to purchase land in the vicinity of Wood Lane and George Street. Mr. Mason pointed out that "the present cemetery at Old Fallow was altogether out of the way as far as the people of Hednesford were concerned and it was a great hardship for people who wished to visit the graves of loved ones that they should have to travel so far". Remember the graveyard would be for those not of Anglican or Catholic faith. Catholics could only bury their dead at Cannock (a graveyard for Hednesford Catholics would not appear until 1935). The vicar at St. Peter's said that the graveyard at the church was sufficient.

February Hednesford was rocked by the horrific murder of Elizabeth Gaskin by her husband, Thomas, on February 19th. The funeral took place on March 2nd performed by Stacey's.

*More is written about this in *Murder and Manslaughter around Cannock Chase* by your author or in Paul Bedford's book *Gaskin* where he examines the life stories of both families.

March Mr. Mason gave one acre of land to the Council for the betterment of West Hill Schools "by way of thanksgiving for victory in the War".

August 31st Fire broke out at West Hill School for Girls destroying a lot of the building. More of this episode in *A History of Hednesford and Surrounding Villages* by your author.

November Oil stores adjoining the Pumping Station on the Rugeley Road were completely gutted by fire. It appeared that an employee visited the stores at about 9.00 p.m., but stoutly denied having matches, pipe or tobacco in his possession. He locked the doors securely and left, but about fifteen to twenty minutes later the workmen were alarmed by a loud explosion and the sight of flames coming from the stores. Racing to the scene the workmen managed to put the fire out and save three nearby cottages. The cost of the damage was around £150. Fire brigades from Cannock or Lichfield did not attend.

28. Pumping Station c.1905.

The Post War Years
(1920 - 1929)

1920

January Government Inspectors complained about the condition of Rawnsley School concerning lack of repairs, heating and "sanitary offices" (the toilets). Apparently £91 had been spent on the building in **1914**, though no record of it existed in the log book. Fires were lit every morning at 6 o'clock, but in winter they proved insufficient (even the ink in the inkwells froze solid!). As to the sanitary offices, just before the inspectors arrived, the water supply had been cut off and the janitor had to carry water from a nearby farm. In addition the children were terrified of rats in the ashpit. The headmaster, Mr. Barratt, stated that only w.c.'s would solve the problem, but the problem with that was there was no drainage from the site and the Council had failed to obtain land for a sewage farm.

29. Rawnsley School.

The school got running water in **1915**, but it was not until **1927** that it had flush toilets. In **1930** the school had electricity.

January Because of the War industries like brick making had suffered and had led to a shortage of bricks to build houses. To solve the problem the Council bought huts from Brocton Camp at £80 each, but by the April it decided to purchase steel framed houses instead.

February/July/August Fires continued to be major cause for concern in the area. On **Tuesday February 10th** the Colliery Institute (the Stute) at Rawnsley was gutted by fire, the damage estimated at £3,000. On **July 17th** an oil store at East Cannock Colliery was gutted. The Cannock Fire Brigade, on its way to help Hednesford's Brigade, led by Mr. Jos. Payton, had an accident. Two horses pulling the engine along Church Street at a gallop failed to negotiate a rather sharp turn into Hednesford Road and were dashed into the wall and fencing in front of Mr. Colley's house. Their speed carried them and the front part of the engine into the garden. Fred Marshall, the driver, was thrown on top of the horses while three other men were thrown to the ground. Fortunately no one was hurt, even the horses. Finally on **August 7th** the colliery hay stores at West Cannock Colliery were gutted and two sheds and about 60 tons of hay were destroyed, costing well over £1,000.

May/June Meetings were held to discuss the provision of a memorial for those who had died in the war. It was decided that "a public memorial be erected by public subscription" and "take the form of a monument surmounted by a cross and that the Marquis of Anglesey be approached for the necessary land on the Hills".

*More can be discovered in the booklet *In Proud Thanksgiving* on sale at the Museum of Cannock Chase or from The Friends of the Museum of Cannock Chase – Local History Society.

November Littleworth Tileries were taken over by Fields Ltd. of London and Peterborough and promised new extensions. Those extensions were finally to come in the 1950's done by the Midland Division of the Coal Board. They raised production by 50% from 16 to 24 million bricks per annum.

Historical note – Hednesford brick making had long been in the area. As early as the 1830's Francis Foulk had his brickyard up today's Littleworth Road and on his death it was taken over by Thomas Cotton.

1921

May 2nd A memorial clock was placed on the wall of Hednesford Progressive Club overlooking Market Street along with a bronze plaque inlaid with enamel to honour those club members who gave their lives in the War. It was Hednesford's first clock in the main street.

30. Market Street c.1910.

Those honoured were as follows:-

Lieutenant Edwin Gwyther; F. Hammond; James W. Holmes; J.H. Hornblower; Aaron Jones; W. Owen Kilgallon; John Lewis; Sergeant James Mottram; Frank Reynolds; Albert Richardson; William Rogers; Leonard Slade; Jack Smith; and Frank Suthard.

May Underground telephone wires were to be laid in Market Street, but only after the Council got assurance from the Company that they would repair any damage done to the newly tarmaced road. At the same meeting the Council were informed of the lack of privies in houses in Platt Street, as well as other streets. They gave the owners six weeks to install water closets and insisted that Platt Street should be "sewered".

July 9th Yet another fire broke out, that time at the Wagon Works in Station Road. The large wooden workshop on the Rugeley side of Hednesford Station, together with eleven trucks and many tools were completely destroyed. Damage was estimated at £6,000.

31. Wagon Works, Hednesford c.1920.

Meanwhile on the Friday night men playing cricket on Rawnsley Field spotted a hay rick belonging to Cannock and Rugeley Company on fire. Cannock Fire Brigade was called, but the rick was destroyed at a cost of £200.

December The Electricity Scheme – Cables were going to be laid from Wolverhampton to Cannock. As for Hednesford the Council said that "the residents and shopkeepers there must make a requisition to the Council for the supply and then steps would be taken to meet their demand".

1922

April Electricity supply to Hednesford – As to the shops in Market Street and Station Road the Council would very soon comply "if the tradesmen came along with their orders". As to the houses in the area "the Council would like to supply all houses with electricity".

Historical note:- Your author's house was built in 1926 and was lit by gas!

April High Town School was finally opened.

September The Wesleyan Methodist Chapel on Station Road held its Jubilee celebrations.

October 7th/14th Hednesford Shopping Week began. Traders had decorated their windows and the event began with a pageant through the town. Decorated cars, cycles and trucks headed the parade followed by Cannock Fire Brigade with their new engine. On Tuesday evening boxing contests were held at the Drill Hall, while on Thursday a "King Carnival" was crowned at the Electric Palace. On Thursday afternoon some 2,000 watched a football match at the Cross Keys between Aston Villa and West Bromwich Albion junior teams. (Hednesford had close links with both clubs having supplied them with many good players over the years.)

32. Hednesford Carnival c.1920.

33. Inset, the front cover of Hednesford Shopping Week Magazine.

November 9th Hednesford's War Memorial was opened by Countess Alice of Athlone. ★More can be found in *A History of Hednesford and Surrounding Villages* by your author.

1923

February 24th A meeting of the Hednesford & District War Memorial Committee met at the Soldiers Institute to consider the deficit regarding the cost of the memorial which was £347 10s 4d. The bazaar held during the week of the opening made £200 less than expected despite the ladies' hard work. Further ideas were needed to raise money. They included a draw, a garden party and another appeal or letter asking for further subscriptions.

The memorial itself had been fully paid for, but more was needed for improvements to the recreation grounds. The working men's clubs had been asked to supply seats and had agreed, but 500 silver birch needed to be planted in the grounds. Unfortunately some damage had occurred, done by children, and the police were to be asked to keep an eye on the premises. For the first time it was suggested that the Council could be asked to take over the maintenance.

June A club for ex-servicemen was purchased from Old Brocton Camp (it had previously been the cinema) to be placed at the Soldiers Institute in Anglesey Street.

November Bus routes were to be added to Pye Green and Rawnsley, but before they could operate the roads had to be repaired. Part had been done at a cost of £7,000.

1924

January Street lamps were to be erected for Green Heath where there was "a mile of streets without a single lamp". Electric or gas? Gas was preferred "if the Gas Company agreed to light them at half rate for the remainder of the season (until May)". High Town still had no street lights!

May The Council proposed to widen Market Street, but first had to acquire a portion of the Anglesey lawn. The

34. War Memorial c.1930.

Hednesford members of the Council had met with Messrs. Roberts Brewery and had been informed that the Marquis of Anglesey needed to approve the exclusion of the portion of land from the brewery lease. The extent would be 45 feet from the existing boundary fence. If it went ahead the Council would build a brick dwarf wall with pallisading, but there was to be no other erection on site. In November it was announced that the scheme would start without further delay.

35. Market Street c.1930.

At the same meeting it was decided that alterations to Hednesford Railway Station were needed, but the Railway Company had to do them.

August The question of a water supply to Pye Green. There had been complaints by residents of the poor supply (wells had almost dried up in the summer), but when Mr. G.H. Smith, the sanitary inspector, examined them he found "more water than last year". He also added that "owing to the elevation of Pye Green water supply had been impractical in the past, but if they had electricity in the district something might be done to power water pumps".

Historical note: Eventually a pumping station was built on the Green Heath Road and still stands there today, opposite Florence Street. In 1934 the Water Tower was completed at Pye Green.

36. Water Tower, Pye Green.

1925

May Rawnsley Institute was extended with the addition of a new billiard room opened by Colonel Williamson.

September Hednesford Railway Station improvements? After a discussion with London Midland & Scottish Railway Company the matter was deferred until a more "favourable

37. Bradbury Lane Mission Sunday School Annual March c.1910 (see page 36).

time". There were objections from some councillors who claimed that "the raising of platforms was an urgent matter and should have the immediate attention of the Railway Company. In their present state they were a real danger to passengers alighting from the trains. There had already been several accidents."

October The Electricity question – Should there be a new sub-station at Hednesford? It could be sited at the corner of King Street and Littleworth Road and then be laid 150 yards to Messrs. Field's Tileries, hence feeding King Street and Littleworth Road. The cost would be £1,209 for building and equipment.

October 31st Bradbury Lane Mission (it still stands today as a private house at the bottom of Bradbury Lane) was to be closed for extensions. It reopened in **May, 1927** after they were complete. The right wing of the building was brought level with the frontage and a new pulpit and communion rail added at a total cost of £380 raised by members.

1926

The year was dominated by the General Strike and Hednesford, like many other working class areas, suffered greatly.

On **June 4th** the Hednesford Relief Committee acted to feed the children of those suffering most. Contributions were requested so that 6d per meal per child could be arranged. The distribution centres were to be at St. Saviour's Church room; the Salvation Army Hall; the Wesleyan Schoolroom; Mount Street Congregational Schoolroom; and the Bradbury Lane Wesleyan Mission. Around 1,400 were fed in that way. As the Strike progressed meals were increased to six a week at 1s per child. Gradually the miners drifted back to work (by

38. The following fed children during the Strike at the Salvation Army Hall.
L-R front row- J. Nicholls, Mrs. Nicholls, H. Watkiss, M.A. Foster, H. Bishop, B. Garbett.
Middle row - G. Stokes, E. Bellam, H. Watkiss, Mrs. Haycock, A. Gough, H. Martin, Mrs. Handy, Mrs. Croppers. Back row - B. Jones, J. West, J. Moulden.

39. Coal picking at Wimblebury Colliery during the Strike.

mid–August some 5,000 were back) and the Committee, through lack of funds, dropped the meals to four a week. The fund was finally closed in the October.

Others fed the children. In the Cross Keys area of Hednesford the Old Hednesford Wesleyan Mission in Hill Street provided meals for about 120 children as often as they could, while Mrs. Vernon of Old Hednesford Post Office gave tea to about 250 mothers and children on June 17th.

40. Children fed at Salvation Army Hall.

41. Soup kitchen at St. John's.

July Brindley Village got its working men's club which was opened on Wednesday July 28th through the generosity of West Cannock Colliery Company who converted one of the hospital huts which had been a dining room. The new club had five rooms, including a smoke room, a reading room, a bar and a billiard room, in addition to a concert hall. While the Colliery Company met the cost of the conversion the members would have to furnish it.

When the hospital closed down in **May, 1923** West Cannock Colliery Company bought the site to house some of its workers. After renovation every house contained electricity and a bathroom and had plenty of land for gardening. An up-to-date sewerage system was constructed and South Staffs Water Company provided running water to every dwelling. By **1926** there were 31 families in the village and by **1929** that had extended to about 60 families. The village already had a church and a school and would become a thriving community. For more on Brindley Village see the author's book *A History of Hednesford and Surrounding Villages.*

December A proposed new local railway. Part of the scheme included a light railway line from Brindley Heath, Hednesford to Wrottesley, a distance of about 12 miles. It would pass under Bradbury Lane, Mount Side Street, Heath Street, Green Heath Road and over Belt Road by means of a bridge, over Princess Street by a crossing, under Cemetery Road, Old Fallow Road, Pye Green Road and Stafford Road before heading on to Wrottesley. The idea was to facilitate the movement of mineral traffic and had been suggested on several occasions before.

Plans and costs (amounting to £522,640) had been drawn up and the Government would be petitioned. Those plans were rejected in **May, 1927**. *Fortunately for your author as my house in Mount Street stands very close that proposed line!

1927

The Sunday Observance question surfaced again with the Electric Palace wanting to have cinema shows. The Council refused, but did allow concerts instead.

★Children's matinees began in the August at the Electric Palace, closely followed by afternoon sessions at Hednesford Picture Palace (The Forum) on the Rugeley Road, costing 1d. I can still vividly remember droves of us kids watching Flash Gordon and the like in the 1940's on a Saturday morning! The cheering for our hero and the booing of Emperor Ming still echoes in my memory.

June 14th Disaster struck at Wimblebury Colliery when the cage carrying nineteen men went out of control. Fourteen men were injured, but fortunately no one was killed. More of this incident can be found in *A History of Hednesford and Surrounding Villages.*

July 23rd Yet another fire in Hednesford; that time at a sweets and refreshment shop in Cannock Road occupied by Mr. Ephraim Jones, an elderly invalid. Mr. Payton, Hednesford's chief fire officer, was quickly on the scene and attached the hose to the hydrant in Cannock Road. Meanwhile the police, called from the Police Station just along the road, rescued Mr. Jones. The shop was gutted and damage estimated at £150.

November A meeting of the Hednesford War Memorial Committee, whose job it had been to look after the maintenance of the memorial and grounds, decided to ask the Council to take over its responsibility as they had done with Cannock's memorial.

November The Prince of Wales played golf at Beaudesert and noticed Coulthwaite's horses being trained on the Chase. It wasn't long before he was sending his own horses to Coulthwaite's stables.

1928

January Throughout their history shops had been able to regulate their own hours, but the Council decided to change that. In future all shops had to close at 8.00 p.m. other than on late days (Friday and Saturday) and early closing day (in Hednesford that was Thursday). Tobacconists were allowed to stay open until 9.30 p.m.

The exceptions were as follows:- 1. Sales of meals consumed on the premises. 2. Sales of newly cooked provisions. 3. Medicines. 4. Newspapers and books. 5. Sale of motor, cycle or aircraft accessories for immediate use. 6. The Post Office. 7. Sales at bazaars or fairs.

42. Prince of Wales with Tom Coulthwaite.

February West Cannock No 4 Pit finally closed. Just north of West Cannock No. 1 on Green Heath Common it was also opened in 1869.

★I do not propose to give a history of each pit in the area as it closed as the book *The Cannock Chase Coalfield and its Coal Mines* by the Cannock Chase Mining Historical Society says it all. They have also produced books on the various mines and companies.

June 28th In the late **1870's** Pye Green Primitive Methodist Church was built with the expectation that the population would grow. However, it had not and the church had fallen into disrepair. Consequently about five years ago land was acquired on the corner of Florence Street and Green Heath Road to build a new one. With the money from the sale of the old church (£130) and subscriptions the stone laying ceremony took place. The two principal stones were laid by Mr. Lloyd of Stafford and Mr. Tom Mason of Hednesford who was the only surviving member of the original trustees of the Pye Green Church.

The new church would serve as a Sunday School and would be built in brick with a slate roof. The body of the church would be 45 ft by 25ft and would provide seating for around 250 people. Two vestries were being provided and a heating chamber. There was also sufficient land for later extensions. The total cost of the materials and furnishings was estimated at £850 with £639 13s 10d already collected.

In **June, 1954** a new church hall was built, the land being purchased from the Teddesley Estate for £235. The ground for the hall was subsequently levelled by the men and youths from the church. The total cost of the clearance and erection was £412.

Historical note – The old Pye Green Methodist Chapel became a club known as "Ye Old Birds" in the early 1940's and remained as such until it became "The Birds" later in the century. It was finally closed and later demolished in 2014. Houses now stand on the site.

July Cannock Chase Miners' Association were recommended by their sub-committee to acquire the 16 and a half acres of land known as the Old Pool, between Rugeley Road and Victoria Street with a view to its being converted into a recreation ground and park. By October they had purchased it and decided it was to be a park.

August 7th Brindley Village held its annual sports event, proving that the village was a thriving community. In the evening a fancy dress carnival and dance was held in the Village Hall.

★For anyone interested in the Village's history and people the sports results and much more appeared in the *Cannock Advertiser* at the time.

October Yet another meeting of the Memorial Committee wanted to hand over the maintenance to the Council, but there was a legal hitch – the land, given by the Marquis of Anglesey, had never been legally given to the trustees. They had no deeds to the land to give the Council and to get those would cost £20. At that time they had an overdraft of £5 6s 6d.

November Hednesford Brook which still runs today under Market Street and down to East Cannock pools opposite the Stagborough Way Estate was causing problems, but the Council decided that it was the responsibility of the property owners to keep the culvert clear and maintain it. Does that still apply today?

43. War Memorial c.1935.

1929

January The Prince of Wales was again at Hazel Slade that time visiting Coulthwaite's stables and the Flaxley Green training ground.

February Widening of Old Hednesford Road – The Unemployment Grants Committee (the National one) had offered to give the Council 75% of the cost provided 75% of the workforce was taken from the Walsall Employment Exchange and started before March 4th. The Council wanted it done as early as 1921 because it needed a new bus route to take congestion from the Chadsmoor route, but Old Hednesford Road had proved too dangerous. The Council decided it was impossible to comply with the suggestion in the timescale because landowners had yet to be consulted. The Government agreed and let the grant hold until the time was suitable.

February The families of Brindley Village asked Lichfield Rural District Council who controlled it if they would light the village and also repair some of the roads which were in a bad condition, especially in wet weather.

April To add to the woes of Hednesford Memorial Committee in late April a fire damaged a large number of trees and shrubs at the site. It was thought to have been started by a spark from a steam engine going along Rugeley Road.

August The funeral of **Mr. W.H. Sheppard** (76) took place. He lived at York House in Anglesey Street and was the first man in Hednesford to own a motor car. Born in Shropshire he came to Hednesford as a youth and was a pioneer of electrical engineering in the district. He later moved to America, but returned to Hednesford around 1900.

December 6th The funeral of **Mr. F.T. Bumstead** took place at St. Luke's, Cannock. He was born in London and was a fellow student at King's College with Mr. N. Chandler with whom he had joint business interests for many years. Both served their apprenticeship at a Glasgow shipyard and between fifty and sixty years ago they came to Cannock. They then founded an engineering firm in 1873 at Hednesford, known as Bumstead and Chandler,

on the Rugeley Road which made things like water pumping equipment for ships. Bumstead was also the inventor of a paper bag making machine.

He took an active part in the public and religious life of the area, for a number of years being a member of the Board of Guardians. He built the New Hall in Anglesey Street, on the same side of the street as the Anglesey Hotel, and at the rear erected an institute for young men, later presented to the area to entertain troops stationed at Hednesford. He also constructed a similar building at Chadsmoor, known as the "New Link". For a number of years he owned the Public Rooms at Hednesford (later the Picture House) where he provided billiard tables.

44. Uriah Rosson at Bumstead & Chandler.

He was chief layman in Cannock Parish and for almost thirty years was the vicar's warden at St. Luke's. He was also a great benefactor of St. Luke's and St. Chad's as well as other local churches and founded a mission in Old Fallow Road. He became a J.P. in 1908 and rarely missed a court session. He was also Chairman of the local Nursing Association. He helped in organising the Jubilee and coronation celebrations, mainly dealing with the elderly and young.

Very interested in scientific progress and its value to society he got experts to come and give lectures on matters like telegraphy. He inaugurated the first public omnibus service in the area and had a motor built to his own design and that he used to run between Cannock and the White Lion at Huntington. In his younger days he loved horses and was a good sailor and keen yachtsman.

He was buried in Hatherton Churchyard along with his wife who had died on February 19th, 1925.

What's Round the Corner
(1930 - 1939)

1930

February Plans were proposed to improve Victoria Street which would be levelled, metalled, channelled and generally made good at a cost of £1495 8s 9d. They were approved, but as to the widening and reconstruction of Old Hednesford Road from the bridges to Hill Top it was decided to defer it until a later date.

March Hednesford Traders met to revive the old association which had fallen into disuse owing to lack of interest. Mr. Holland told the meeting that the old association had promoted Hednesford by advertising and persuading I. and N.M. Rly Company to run a bus service to Hednesford. However, "if they did not wake up they would find, sooner than they liked, that Hednesford would become a back number simply because there was a lack of interest in the town apart from what they found at the back of their own counters". Mr. Stanton, the chairman, agreed and it was decided to set up a new Chamber of Commerce.

There was also at the same time grumblings about Hednesford's rate money being spent in Cannock at a meeting in Eskrett Street Working Men's Club. A Council reply by a Hednesford Councillor showed those rumblings to be misplaced as in the total Council budget Hednesford had £18,288 spent on it while Cannock only had £17,129. Hednesford's expenditure had included Market Street Crescent; kerbing and improvement to Rugeley Road; Uxbridge Street; Belt Road improvements; Foster Avenue and Pye Green Road sewerage; Victoria Street and Rugeley Road sewerage; and Station Road reconstruction. Also 1818 water closets had been substituted for 1643 privies as well as 1204 ashbins for 676 ashpits.

Historical note – for those readers not too sure of the sanitation in the area at the time most houses were not connected to the main sewers and "waste" went into a pit at the back of the houses and every now and then a cart arrived to empty the pit. In fact the group of houses where I lived as late as the 1940's on the common above Heath Street still had a sewer pit.

Thomas Mason died. He was born in Hinckley, Leicestershire in 1850. He learned his trade as a bricklayer with his father who owned a small business in Wolverhampton and after a few years left to go to London and got a position with Mr. T. Ireland of Notting Hill as a copsin. He returned to Staffordshire at the age of 28 and settled in Hednesford in partnership with his brother, Fred, as builders. Fred later went to Australia and started the work of a fruit grower and contractor. Thomas remained and expanded the business in Hednesford which was a growing town at the time. He moved to Fair Mount on Station Road and set up his builder's yard (today's Michael Bradford's Accountancy firm).

Over the years he carried out a great deal of private and public work. He built police stations at Darlaston, Stone and Tettenhall as well as schools at Stafford and five blocks around Walsall Wood and Chase Terrace. Locally he enlarged the Chadsmoor Schools, built the Heath Hayes Schools and the Infirmary at Cannock Workhouse. He also worked on the enlargement of Gentleshaw Church. His work was thought so highly of that Lord Hatherton spoke very well of him.

45. St. John's Trustees. L - R, back row W. Dunning, J. S. Kendrick, R. D. Stanton, C. F. Gellion, E. W. Haden, J. H. Lowery, J. Hindley and W. D. Wright. L - R front row, P. H. Jones, M. Wright, S. J. Stanton, Rev. A. Stirzaker, T. Mason, W. Mason and J. Hindley.

Apart from his business Thomas played a large part in local government having been on the old Local Board since April, 1890. He continued with that when it became Cannock Chase District Council of which he was chairman and vice-chairman on several occasions. For six years he served as one of the Guardians of the Poor and for several years he was a member of Lichfield Rural Council serving for Hazel Slade. He had also taken more than a layman's share in local religious work, being a founder member of St. John's Methodist Church in Station Road, Hednesford and a trustee for many years. He was also one of the superintendents of the church and was a vice-president of the Free Church Council.

June Sunday Observance – After a long heated debate it was decided to open the council playing fields on a Sunday, but the apparatus and equipment should be locked away and there were to be no organised games permitted. Reverend A. Stirzaker objected stating he did not think "that compromising by opening at 3.30 p.m. on Sundays was any good at all. His parishioners at the Wesleyan Church thought it a retrograde step. If the children went to Sunday School and from there straight to the recreation grounds the ideals which they had tried to inculcate would be rapidly wiped out."

1931

January The Council decided 1. The Miners' Welfare Committee were to be allowed to build a wall and fix a fence along the supposed new road line on Rugeley Road in front of the tennis courts and bowling green (still there today). The park boundary was to be considered at a later date with view to widening Rugeley Road. 2. Whieldon buses were to be allowed to run along Old Hednesford Road. 3. Land for a tip at Green Heath Road was to be purchased from the Ecclesiastical Commission.

April On April 2nd the Government introduced the Sunday Performance Bill in which it permitted councils the right to grant licenses for the purpose of musical entertainment, cinematography, exhibitions and debate. Strangely stage plays were excluded. However, it did say that councils had to have the approval of a great majority of their citizens before they could act. Cinemas in particular had to give a percentage of their Sunday profits to charity and no person could be employed on the Sunday who had already worked six days that week.

April Road widening at East Cannock – The trustees of the Roman Catholic School at Hill Top (St. Joseph's) were prepared to make a grant of 110 square yards of land providing the Council would 1. Erect a wall or fencing along the whole frontage of the school (it's still there); 2. The school had no liability for charges; and 3. The school was allowed to build new rooms as per plan submitted.

Discussions also included the reconstruction of the road from Littleworth Road to Piggott Street, Wimblebury (now Scott Street).

June 14th The worst storm on record hit the Cannock Chase area on Sunday afternoon. At the Cross Keys Hotel a Scouts and Guides rally was flooded out and Mr. Parkinson, the landlord, packed as many as he could into the hotel. The grounds around were flooded to a depth of two to three feet and scouts, police and others rescued children from the water. Water from the main road outside flooded into the passage, bar and other rooms while the cellar was under water.

At Church Hill water poured off Hednesford Hills, bringing with it tons of mud and stones. The embankment on the left-hand side had a large hole torn in it, dangerously close to some houses and foundations of some buildings were left unsafe. On the Littleworth side of the Hills a huge wall was pushed over and portions of the footpath were washed into the Tileries pool.

At West Hill the water poured down into Hednesford like a river, bringing with it footpaths and kerbstones. Big holes were left in some roads and gardens, notably in the West Hill School's gardens. The result of the flow down West Hill and Church Hill meeting at the bottom of Market Street resembled a whirlpool. Hednesford Garage got the full force and cars were covered up to their radiators, with a motor cycle completely submerged. So great was the force of the water that the earth swept away left a ten foot drop from the main road to the entrance to the garage.

46. *Storm damage on Church Hill in 1931.*

Dr. Smith's house, the "Lowlands", was flooded, the gardens and driveway suffering most. Tranters butchers' shop had its cellar flooded and Holland's draper's shop had stock ruined. The East Cannock Road was flooded (but that happened yearly near the bridges) while outside the West Cannock Colliery Offices on Cannock Road it resembled a lake.

Lightning struck many houses including Alfred Taylor's house in Bradbury Lane, where the chimney collapsed damaging the roof and widows; a bungalow in Wimblebury occupied by Mr. G. Bates and belonging to Cannock and Rugeley Colliery Company (the railway house); and the "White House" at Brindley Heath occupied by Mr. Dunford. The lightning also caused severe shock to residents in Bradbury Lane and Station Road.

Finally water flowed "like the River Trent" down West Cannock Colliery sidings towards Hednesford Station carrying with it rails, sleepers and ballast. From 6.00 p.m. on the Sunday evening some 200 to 300 men worked to repair it until by the Tuesday it was all cleared. Fortunately the pit workings did not suffer.

Historical note – **Bill Harvey** remembers the storm well. He was at the Drum Head Service at the Cross Keys when it began. "My brother, Jack, was Cross Bearer for St. Peter's Choir and what a task he had with it. Scared stiff of the lightning, we wrapped the cross up in his choir robes and went up Hill Street and Wood Lane to our house in George Street. When we got there my dad's cabbage plants, which he had only just planted out, were being swept out of the house by my mother. There was more soil in the house than in the garden. Half of Church Hill ended up in Market Street and had to be carried away by horse and cart before Blagg's Corner was usable again."

While **Harold Evans** says, "After leaving Sunday School at the Wesleyan Chapel I walked down the town to attend the service at the Cross Keys. A few spots of rain were falling, but by the time I got to Uxbridge Street they were the size of half crowns and so I sheltered in Blagg's doorway. The rain came down like a torrent and flowed down Church Hill bringing with it sand, gravel and even kerbstones. When it stopped the town was under water and so I rolled up my trousers and set off to paddle home, passing Jones' Music Shop where pianos were floating in the showroom. Dr. Mitchell's wife, wearing fishermen's waders, was rescuing stranded children.

1932

January It was proposed to transfer control of Hazel Slade from Lichfield Rural District Council to Cannock Urban Council. It was eventually agreed and by the December it was also proposed that electricity should be taken to the village.

January The Accident Home at Hednesford had largely survived on the generosity of the local miners who contributed 1d per week from their wages. 6d was also collected from

47. Accident Home 1907.

them about 8 times a year to support other hospitals like Wolverhampton Royal. (Remember there was no free Health Service in those days). It was suggested that in future the men should contribute 3d per week plus 1d for the Accident Home. It was also hoped that a share of the 3d per week could go to the Accident Home which was in need of repair. In February there was also a report on the Miners' Home in Weston Super Mare. In **March 1933** a report stated that the Home was in need of repair because of cracked walls.

March It was proposed to build 102 new houses at Pye Green which only had 50 parlour type houses. Questions were asked about possible subsidence and the possibility of a bus route. In **January 1933** it was decided to build just 50 new houses, but care had to be taken if West Cannock Colliery Company decided to mine under them. However, they were told that "many years would elapse before there would be workings under those properties". They were under construction by the March and in September 1933 it was decided to build another 52 by direct labour.

March/August Hednesford Park was proving very popular with income from the tennis courts being very good (3498 games had been played) while bowls was also popular with 5232 games. The trees, shrubs and plants were doing well as were the bedding plants in the greenhouse. The putting green was not yet in use, but two football pitches were ready for use that season. There had only been one application to use the cricket pitch and the children's playground had yet to be done.

June Hednesford's Chamber of Commerce met to discuss the tip on Green Heath Road. Mr. Bird complained that the Council were tipping far too close to the road and spoiling the only road to Cannock Chase. The area was already blighted by coal tips and if its use remained then the tip would be well above the height of the road in places. He suggested the Council be asked to find a better site. The Chamber suggested he write to the Ministry of Health.

1933

January Colonel Robert Summerside Williamson died on January 16th and was buried at Gentleshaw Church aged 74. He had come to the area with his father in 1868 and taken up residence in Cannock Wood House (later The Grange). He became a member of the Institute of Mining Engineers and Institute of Civil Engineers in 1881 and was president of the South Staffordshire and Warwickshire branch from 1896 to 1898. He was also a member of the Board of Mining Examinations and gave valuable evidence to the Royal Commissions on Mines in the early 1900's. In 1901 he took over from his father as general manager of the Cannock and Rugeley Colliery Company and was a director of the West Cannock and Harrison's Colliery companies.

Always conscious of the safety of the men employed in the industry he was a firm believer in the best machinery and tools for that industry and so gained their respect. He played a large part in the Cannock Chase Mines Rescue Committee being its chairman for many years; added to that he was also involved in the running of the Hednesford Accident Home as well as the home at Weston Super Mare. As chairman of the Hazel Slade Building Company he launched a scheme whereby several hundred miners' homes were built in the district.

Apart from his activities with mining and its welfare he had interest in schemes for the provision of playing fields in the area and in the Rawnsley and Hazel Slade districts he involved himself in old folks treats, hospital work and religious movements as well as the provision for recreation of young people. To aid those interests he was a member of Cannock Urban District Council, being the second chairman appointed. He was also a keen sponsor of Rawnsley Flower Show and the Rawnsley Institute as well as St. Michael's bazaars.

He joined the old Volunteer Force and the Territorials in 1881 when its headquarters were supposed to be in Cannock, but lack of interest saw them removed to Hednesford where they stayed. The Volunteers had just gone into scarlet uniforms when he joined and were the first battalion in the county to have the khaki uniforms. He was appointed to the command of the company in 1887/88 and in 1901 was in command of the battalion. At first the only place for drill was Anglesey Field, but in 1894 he called the people of the area together and seeing the need for a drill hall they subscribed

48. Colonel R. S. Williamson.

enough for the Drill Hall to be built. He finally resigned command in 1913. In 1914 he took up command of the local Volunteers and in 1920 resumed command of his old battalion, but finally retired in 1922.

Apart from those many activities in his private life he was a keen dog and poultry breeder and had some success at national shows. He was also a keen cricketer, being a good bowler, and was captain of the Cannock and Rugeley Colliery Team for several years. Another great interest was the Scout Movement and be became a District Commissioner. When he died he left a widow, but no children.

April At a meeting of the Hednesford Thursday Cricket Club dissatisfaction was expressed about the "unfinished park" while Cannock Park, which had started later, was more advanced. Also there was a good deal of complaint in Hednesford about the lack of the children's playground. Plans had been submitted to the Miner's Welfare Council and they were awaiting the money. In **January, 1935** the work on the children's playground was finally started, though modified, and it was also decided to fence off the brook.

April 16 objectors took the Council to court with regards to Mount Street, from High Mount Street upwards, and part of Mount Side Street. The Council claimed it was a private street and not a highway and therefore should be looked after by the owners of the newly built houses (including your author's), but the proposed work to make it proper should be done by council contract and not the owners. Sewers had been put in by private builders and connected to the main ones and the Council had not objected. Those Council sewers had been positioned in the area to service the new Prairie Farm Estate. In 1929 the Council had erected thirty poles to convey electricity, but had no record of asking the owners' permission.

Eighty year old **John Nicholls** of Station Road said he had known the street for fifty seven years. In olden days it was called West Cannock Street and it led straight to Pye Green, but it was an open common. Some of Mount Street (the lower part) had been made good in 1882, but the remainder was merely a track. In 1933 the streets mentioned were still not curbed or channelled.

May Tragedy struck at West Cannock No. 5 Pit when an explosion ripped through the coal face. Three men died instantly while another three died some days later. More of this tragedy can be found in *A History of Hednesford and Surrounding Villages.*

49. Funeral of Benjamin Cornwall killed in the West Cannock No.5 Pit explosion.

May The Marquis of Anglesey sold the Anglesey Hotel to Eley's Brewery, Stafford, part of the Wolverhampton Brewery. At the same time various plots of land, previously part of the hotel land in Anglesey Street, were sold off to local people. The Stanton family also purchased the land on which Moore's factory stood.

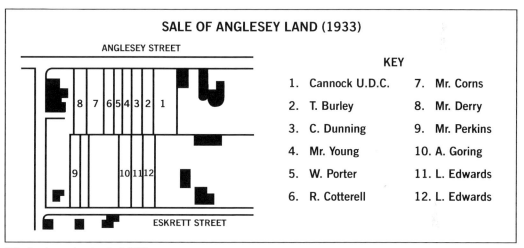

SALE OF ANGLESEY LAND (1933)

ANGLESEY STREET

KEY

1. Cannock U.D.C.	7. Mr. Corns
2. T. Burley	8. Mr. Derry
3. C. Dunning	9. Mr. Perkins
4. Mr. Young	10. A. Goring
5. W. Porter	11. L. Edwards
6. R. Cotterell	12. L. Edwards

ESKRETT STREET

50. Anglesey land sale 1933.

Historical note – In 1872 the then Marquis had leased the hotel to Thomas Eskrett. "The said property was (with other property) by a lease dated November 8th, 1872 made between Henry William George, Marquis of Anglesey, and Thomas Eskrett for a term of 99 years from October 10th, 1872 at a yearly rate of £250." On May 11th, 1876 an underlease was made between Thomas Eskrett and William Henry Moore to rent out Nos. 71, 73 and 75 Market Street where the factory was to stand.

October The body of Nancy Foster was discovered in the canal at East Cannock Basin on Saturday October 28th at 12.30 p.m. by Frank Coleman, a canal worker from East Cannock. She had been missing since the Thursday when she left home to go to work at the West Cannock Colliery Offices. The twenty year old daughter of Mr. & Mrs. S. Foster, who lived at the rear of 22 Market Street, was a writer of poems of great promise about Hednesford and the area. Several poems had been published in periodicals and papers and some had been set to music.

She had attended the West Hill, Belt Road and Centrals Schools and left to become a short hand typist at the West Cannock Offices. However, when she began to have trouble with the nerves in her hand and arm she transferred to a telephone operator. Her father, Samuel, told the inquest, held at Hednesford Rescue Station, that she had been receiving regular treatment for her illness at Wolverhampton Hospital from the January. Though depressed at times she usually recovered quite quickly. Dr. Redmund and Dr. J.G. Mitchell, both of Hednesford, said they had treated her, but thought she would not get better as she was of "a very highly strung nature". Although not in pain her disability stopped her doing various activities.

1934

February The Government proposed to change school leaving age from 14 to 15. While most councillors agreed some argued that a "number of boys in the area who had left school two months ago still had not obtained employment" and those objectors said "it would be better if they were kept at school until they had gained work".

March A new public house was to be built at the junction of Pye Green Road and Belt Road (today's Jubilee). The license would come from the Rose and Crown at Cheslyn Hay. It was much needed because of the building of the Prairie Farm Estate which had been plotted out for 400 houses, a large number of which had already been built. On Belt Road land had been acquired for a further two hundred houses. The road going passed the site was very busy, the Council having introduced a bus route in the area which went around Pye Green and down passed the proposed site. Butler's Brewery, who owned the Rose and Crown, had produced plans for the new inn. The Council granted the application. ★The name Jubilee was chosen to mark George V's Jubilee in 1935.

March Mr. C.A. Lee of Common Farm, Cannock Road died. The farm was opposite today's garage and was one of the oldest farms in the area, being there on the 1841 Tithe Map and lived in by the Benton family. Mr. Lee was born in Bloxwich and came to the farm when he was nine years old. His mother was a Benton and had been born at the farm which had been in the family for over two hundred years. She had died in October, 1933 aged 91 years. The farm eventually disappeared in the late fifties/early sixties.

June 6th Our Lady of Lourdes Catholic Church in Uxbridge Street was opened by Bishop Williams. More of the history can be found in *A History of Hednesford and Surrounding Villages.*

July Prince George visited Cannock Chase on July 21st. At High Town he met members of the Blue Pilgrim Mission and on arriving at Hednesford he visited the Good Companions Home in Anglesey Street before moving on to Wimblebury. Again he met members of the Blue Pilgrim Mission and surprised the children by visiting their school as it was raining hard, saving them from getting a thorough soaking.

Historical note - The Blue Pilgrims were a women's movement (non-religious, but Christian) founded by Beatrice Hankey in 1902 in London to relieve the distress of the poor and unemployed. They wore a plain blue and white frock, blue coat and skirt, blue headdress and carried a bag and stole, knapsack, light mackintosh and umbrella – hence the nickname. They came to our area sometime after 1910 and set up missions at High Town and

51. Our Lady of Lourdes 1935.

Wimblebury. The story has it that Beatrice was looking for some "strike area" to help those affected. She went to the railway station and simply asked to go to one such area. It just so happened that the clerk came from Gentleshaw and so she came to our area. They worked with distressed miners' families providing food, clothing and money gifts and at first she stayed with the families. The Pilgrims finally opened a place in High Town in conjunction with Harold Dunning who used to supply free milk to the poor. In 1934 their wooden hut at High Town was to be used by the Collier Comrades and Young Pioneers and Homemakers and by 1957 was known as the Pilgrim's Homemakers Hall.

They also had a place in Anglesey Street for out of work miners to go and have a mug of tea, cake and play some games.

August The Bumstead and Chandler Factory was to open again after a Bilston firm had taken over half of the premises and was negotiating to take over the remainder when gas and electricity had been installed.

Historical note – Diamond Wedding of Mr. and Mrs. James Turner of 44 Albert Street, Church Hill in June. He was born at Cannock Wood on Match 17th, 1851 and she was born at Littleworth 80 years ago. They were married at St. Peter's.

Memories of **James Turner** – He started work aged eleven with Cannock Chase Colliery Company working at the Plant Pit and later with Cannock and Rugeley Colliery Company. He only attended school for twelve months and his parents had to pay 3d per week for him to attend. Mrs. Turner, who was born close to where the Accident Home stands, only did nine months at school and went into service aged eleven in Birmingham. His father worked for the Marquis of Anglesey as a gamekeeper. The Marquis was an excellent shot, some days shooting as many as 70 rabbits and 200 pheasants. A generous man to his tenants he often held suppers for them and at Christmas gave each one a piece of beef weighing ten to twelve pounds.

The cottage Mr. Turner had was once used by the Wesleyans for services and was over a hundred years old. He saw the old ruins on Castle Hill unearthed in 1864. Walking over Hednesford Hills he saw few houses, no St. Peter's, and the only ones of note being Lee's Farm and the Anglesey Hotel. He remembered the building of the Uxbridge Hotel to replace the old Blue Pump House. He also remembered Hednesford Pool where lots of fishing took place. When it was drained Colonel Williamson took some fish and put them into a pool at Rawnsley. He also witnessed the Military Manoeuvres on the Hills in 1873 and crowds came from the Black Country to watch, being charged 5 shillings for a place on a vehicle.

1935

January The graveyard at St. Peter's, Church Hill was becoming over-crowded and permission was sought to possibly use some of the Hills as an extension. Also permission was sought to remove grass from the Hills to cover existing graves.

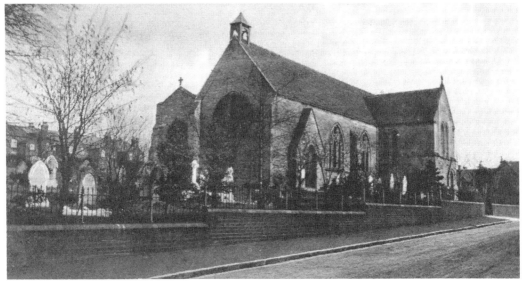

52. St. Peter's Church.

February The Council was asked if Mr. A.J. Pace could be granted permission to build 100 new houses on the Belt Road area.

March Chamber of Commerce member, Mr. S. J. Stanton, arguing about the need for improvements to Hednesford said he had lived there for forty five years and remembered it when only two or three shops were lighted properly. Most were limited to one small lamp and one only had two candles. People used to go about with lanterns and candle light. People also objected when asked to pay for sewerage to the main street. He also remembered when walking from the Cross Keys into Hednesford there was no metalling or curbing of roads and large stones had been placed on the side of the roads to stop carts from going on to the footpaths. Finally he remembered a meeting held at the Public Rooms on Rugeley Road where not one person was in favour of electricity.

April Hednesford Hills Reservoir had stood empty for years and Councillor Wright suggested that it be used some times as a sports arena. South Staffs. Waterworks Company needed to give permission or possibly sell it.

May The Jubilee Celebrations – The day began with a parade, headed by the Salvation Army Band, to St. Peter's Church where a service was held. In the local schools children were given a tea and celebration mugs were presented. Afterwards they went to Hednesford Park where at least seven thousand people congregated to celebrate with dance and music.

June In Wimblebury on Wednesday June 5th there was a ceremony to open the new bowling green and gardens, which had been laid by local men, at the Pilgrim Home. It was in 1912 that Pilgrim Help first arrived in Wimblebury and set up a home in a small cottage. Over the years it was the scene of many happy meetings and in 1926 Pilgrim Help returned to begin the building of the new Home.

August The question of Sunday Observance came up again. Since the new park at Hednesford had been completed the Council wanted to open it to games of tennis, bowls and also open the children's playing fields. It brought strong reaction from many religious groups and societies who still maintained that Sunday was a day of rest. The Council voted 12 to 2 against opening on Sunday for games.

November Hednesford Railway Bridge – Mr. Wright told the Hednesford Chamber of Commerce that there was a plan at the Council to reconstruct the bridge and widen the footpath and the County Council, who were responsible for the road as far as the Anglesey Hotel, had approved the scheme. However, the cost was the problem and the railway company could not be expected to bear it fully. As it was the bridge was dangerous with a footpath which was too small and stationary traffic outside the station caused jams. The matter was again discussed in January, 1936 Mr. Benton adding, "If a woman was on the path carrying a basket it was impossible for anyone to pass without stepping on to the road."

Again in **October** the Chamber complained, adding that the station itself was "a very dismal and dingy place" and shunting should be done outside the station and not inside while people waited for a train.

★The discussion was to go on for many years to come!

For the first time in **1937** the traders voiced their concern about the dangerous condition of the railway bridge at the bottom of Bradbury Lane.

53. Railway bridge looking to West Hill.

54. Station platform Hednesford c.1910.

Historical note – The station bridge had been built in 1874 because in 1873 the Army Manoeuvres on the Chase had meant that the platforms had to be extended. Development on the West Hill side of Hednesford meant that a safe crossing had to be erected over the railway line.

1936

Historical note – **Mr. George Mellor** died in February. He had arrived in Hednesford in 1866 when he was ten years old. His father had built a house in Station Road and he remembered it as "just a cart track with rushes growing two foot high on both sides. There were only four houses there and the land cost just 3d per square yard to buy." He had a coach building business which he ran with his family next to the house and it continued well into the twentieth century.

June It was decided to extend the schools at Littleworth with two new schools. Linford's put in for the contract.

June Once again Hednesford and district was hit by severe thunderstorms. Rainwater gushed down Church Hill and West Hill and met in Market Street opposite "The Lowlands" owned by Dr. Stooke. Both streams brought with them tons of dirt and stones, as much as eight inches thick in places. Residents of Station Road and McGhie Street were flooded out. One of the biggest sufferers was Mr. Pointon, sweet manufacturer in Cannock Road. His factory at the bottom of an incline was flooded ruining everything and even his garage, where his car was, was under water. The Uxbridge Hotel was also flooded as was the late Howard Ball's shop, next to the alleyway to the brook. Further damage was avoided by the action of Mr. Tranter who went up and down the street making sure sewers were kept clear of debris. ★Tradesmen were furious demanding the Council add another sewer to the town near Church Hill.

September Hednesford was to get two new industries 1. The unoccupied parts of the old Bumstead and Chandler factory was to be used for edge tool making (Bestmore's). Also the old established firm of D. Lockett and Sons was to take over a part of the works. Regent's Castings had already had a section of the building for two years. 2. A new factory would be built after Christmas where the old "Manager's home" stood with a frontage to Bate's Corner for glove making. It would employ 100 girls. If that failed then S. Greatrix and Son of Walsall would take over.

Historical note – **Mary Furnell** (nee Craddock) lived in the "Foundry House" which was divided into three – Craddocks, Spooners and Franks. She remembered the foundry when it was owned by Mrs. Best of Cannock. Her maiden name was More, hence Bestmore's Tool and Edge Tool Company. Behind that foundry was Hednesford Wagon Works owned by Mr. Beddows who lived along Station Road, next to Shaw's Garage. Her father was foreman there. There was also an iron foundry there owned by the Hales Brothers who made fire places, grates and fire irons. Finally she remembered a glove making enterprise there also.

The factory was opened in October, 1936 with just a few employees. By 1951 it employed nearly 100, but remained a family business with all family members fully experienced in the edge tool industry. All types of hammers were produced from the stamps and many varied steel stampings were manufactured for the motor, building, carpentry and allied trades. In one year during the Second World War they produced a million hammers for the Ministry of Supply. In addition to those, many components were made for tanks, guns, armoured vehicles, mines and aircraft. A lot of the manual operations had been changed to mechanical ones by the 1950's.

September Would Wimblebury get its own Community Home Centre and in future would it be treated separately from Hednesford when adding new community buildings as "it had always been in the backwater and had missed anything that was going in the way of help"?

December There was a proposal to make Hednesford Post Office a sub office. Cannock should be the centre for the area with the sorting office there and postmen transported to Hednesford. The new postal address for Hednesford would read "Hednesford, Cannock, Staffs." and there would be no post office at Hednesford or official staff. After objections by the Chamber of Commerce it was decided in January, 1937 to have no change in status for the present. *Remember the fuss created when it did finally happen?

December Once again residents complained about the poor lighting of Anglesey Crescent and the town in general. Mr. Lloyd Williams, chemist, said that Cannock was "as well lighted as any place in London" and "everything done for the district seemed to be in Cannock". Mr. Henson said, "If people came into the town any time after lighting-up time it looked dead."

55. Market Street 1917.

Historical note – In contrast **Les Higgs**, local teacher and writer for the local papers in the 1970/80's, published his thoughts of Hednesford when he was a young man in the 1930's. I have paraphrased those thoughts.

Hednesford was small enough for "everybody to know everybody else" and at Christmas there was hardly room outside the Anglesey fence for the Salvation Army to play. In the town many shops had paraffin lamps attached to their fronts. Webster's, Tranter's, Allen's and Jack Ratcliffe's, local butchers, had huge pigs' heads in their windows, each with a Jaffa orange in its mouth. Howell's did a roaring trade in buttons, bows, pretty paper, cards and Christmas crackers. Old W.S. Jones's shop was always filled with people wanting to buy the latest sheet music; while down by Simpson's, the florist, there was always a poor old man singing, "Let the Rest of the World Go By".

56. Map of Hednesford town centre 1938.

The main reason for the crowds was the Market Hall. Inside gaily decorated stalls offered untold bargains. There old man Pointon vied with Harry Poyner to see who could sell the most "sucky fish", humbugs, pineapple drops or little white sugary pigs to put on the Christmas tree.

1937

January The Social Services Movement for Wimblebury, started by Mrs. C. Rowlands, wanted a new building in the village. The Council agreed and it would be of brick foundation with wooden construction of considerable size. It would be centrally heated with a kitchen, reading room and games room and have 6 baths - not all houses had baths! Outside there should be tennis courts and a bowling green. The total cost would be around £1,500. ★That building still stands today, but the outside provisions never happened.

February Because of the condition of many houses in Hednesford, some having been built in the 1870's, the Council had to make plans to remove them on the grounds of health. Owners and some tenants naturally objected. The following were proposed:-

1. Reservoir Road – nos. 35 – 43 and 45 – 55 were considered below standard and subject to subsidence. 2. Mount Street – thirteen houses , five being at the rear of those fronting Mount Street, nos. 59c, 59d, 59e and nos. 61 – 75. 3. In Heath Street 48, 50 and 50a because of disrepair and unfitness. 4. Nine houses in East Cannock Road. 5. Finally Blakemore Street nos. 11 – 23. More proposed clearances were announced in **February, 1938** that time at Rawnsley's nos. 560 – 574.

May Arrangements for the Coronation of Edward VIII – A full programme of events both in Hednesford and Littleworth were arranged including religious services and entertainment. There were fancy dress parades, sports competitions, teas for the children and dances, culminating with a huge bonfire on Hednesford Hills.

May/June At the rear of the shops in Market Street and next to the Rugeley Road, between Uxbridge Corner and the Park, stood a small pool which over the years had become stagnant. It was decided to fill it in and possibly make a car park (Hednesford's first?). Loads of debris was tipped, taking care not to disturb the brook under Market Street. In February, 1939 the Marquis of Anglesey, who owned the lease, objected to the land being used as a car park and it stood for years as empty waste land.

July Hednesford's Carnival was revived after an absence of six years. Harry Johnson of Cradley Heath supplied an ox roast.

57. Ox roast in Hednesford.

1938

March The Station Bridge – New plans were submitted which considered one way traffic, but how did you then get into the town? The bridge near Bradbury Lane was weak due to mining subsidence. An argument broke out at the Council meeting as Hednesford's Chamber of Commerce had been shown the plans before the Council.

March 18th The new Midland Bank opened in Market Street. Today it is a "bookies".

July 78 new houses were to be built in Bradbury Lane with two plots of land being purchased under compulsory order. Also land in Mount Street, owned by Mrs. E. Davies, was to be purchased.

August 25th The Littleworth new schools (one for boys and one for girls) were opened by Mr. W.M. Adamson, M.P. They catered for 320 pupils in each section taken from Heath Hayes, Rawnsley, Wimblebury, Hazel Slade and Hednesford and comprised of five classrooms, two craft rooms and a science room in each school. There were metalwork and woodwork rooms for the

58. Midland Bank after refurbishment.

boys while the girls had laundry rooms. There was also a big assembly hall, containing a stage, and two other large halls. On the north side of the building was a dining room with kitchen, larders and stores. All the buildings were connected by covered walkways and lit by electricity. Finally there was a heated greenhouse to use with the school gardens.

★Notice the sexism of those days. Even stranger to today's thinking was the fact that boys and girls were never allowed to mix. The playground had a painted line down it to denote the two quite separate halves. Beware anyone who crossed over!

September Because of the growing situation in Europe Britain began to prepare. "Everything was done to encourage people to make a little shelter in their garden" and gas masks were made free to the public.

November The first twenty trees were planted in Hednesford Park – "a double rank flanked the footpath from Victoria Street entrance right up to the pavilion".

December The Duke of Kent visited the area, especially Wimblebury where he was delighted by the new Wimblebury Centre and was amazed at what was being done there.

59. Duke of Kent at Hednesford.

1939

As one would expect the prospect of another war was the dominant factor for the year. In April work began on the Hednesford R.A.F. Camp with the "making up" of the old Tackeroo Road. The trains would now stop at Moor's Gorse between Hednesford and Rugeley for the troops. ★The road to the

Camp would be later nicknamed Kitbag Hill. Also there were thoughts of a post office at the Camp. Would the Ministry help with the costs? On the evening of **August 9th** the area had another black-out practise. Despite all that Hednesford went ahead with its Carnival in **July,** but it was marred by heavy rain.

60. Carnival magazine cover 1939.

The War Years and After
(1940 - 1949)

The advent of World War Two saw a new type of warfare which affected civilians as well as troops. Measures to combat possible attack, like the black-out, were nationwide as were rationing, identity cards and the "Dig for Victory" campaign. I do not propose to mention those in detail except where they affected Hednesford in particular, but you will notice that the War did slow down Hednesford's progress.

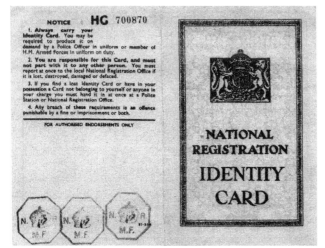

61. Identity card.

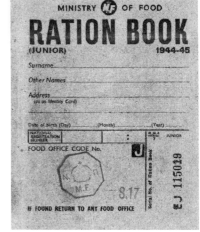

62. Ration book.

1940

March Because of black-out regulations Hednesford shopkeepers decided to alter opening hours to closing at 7 p.m. during the week, with half-day closing on Thursday at 1 p.m. Saturday would be 8 p.m. In winter the hours would be 6 p.m. on weekdays and 7 p.m. on Saturdays.★These hours would not change back after the War and remained until the 1980's.

March It was decided to close Wimblebury Infants School at Easter due to poor sanitary conditions. The managers were not prepared to rebuild the toilets, but merely wanted to repair them. The children would transfer to Heath Hayes.

June Child evacuees arrived in the area. Some 706 children arrived, coming from eighteen coastal towns in the South. 377 arrived at Hednesford Station, the majority being over ten years of age and former pupils of Margate Central Senior Boys School. Locals flocked to the station to welcome them and there was an eagerness on behalf of local people to take the children into their homes. They were firstly taken to the local schools, given a medical check and refreshments and then allocated to the various homes. Most of the boys would attend the new Littleworth School.

July Possible cultivation of unused land was discussed. Hundreds of acres of Hednesford Hills might be ploughed up while the land adjoining the railway at Hednesford Park could also be used. It was also under discussion to plough up parts of the golf course at Beaudesert. ★ None came to fruition.

August Once again the thorny question of Sunday games reared its head. Hednesford Park Bowling Club had started the argument when Mr. William Buckley, the secretary, asked for permission to play its games on a Sunday. There was a protest meeting at St. John's Church, but the Council agreed to allow the games. ★That would be the key for further relaxation in the future.

63. Bowling Club on Anglesey lawn.

1941

January Sunday opening for cinemas? It was argued that Sunday Concerts at churches had been allowed for years and men had to work on Sundays (in the mines) and so why shouldn't the area have other entertainment. Councillor J. Hampton said that the old argument of "If you don't go to church on Sunday then you can't go to the pictures" was wrong. He added, "In years gone by it was considered to be a sin to shave on Sunday." The Council voted 7 – 5 in favour, but adjourned to have a meeting with local religious ministers. In March they reversed their decision by 8 votes to 7, refusing to allow it for the duration of the War at least.

April/May The "Littleworth Lumberjacks" – During the Easter and Whitsun Holidays boys from Littleworth School, including some evacuees, helped with forestry work on Cannock Chase. A group of fifty lads were employed by the Forestry Commission to lop branches and were paid £4 per week and provided with meals and accommodation around the Pottal Pool area. The task was carried out again in 1944. On his visit to the school Lord Harrowby, Lieutenant of the County, praised the boys for their work and later wrote a letter of appreciation.

64. Littleworth lumberjacks - Some of the boys were A. White, G. Searle, K. Pockett and T. Rogers.

October The Duke of Kent visited Littleworth School and witnessed the boys making an extension to their pigsty, gardening and exercising in the gym. He also watched the girls' dance and cookery groups. He was also interested in the school's war effort and was presented with a book explaining the school's work by thirteen year old Alexander White of 239 Station Road. Having left Littleworth he then visited Wimblebury and was shown round the boys' club room and crafts room where he witnessed hand loom weaving. From there he went to see the women's sewing and cookery rooms, finally ending up in the library.

1942

May Again the local cinema owners applied for Sunday opening. They were successful when the Council voted 8 to 4 in favour.

June 29th Hednesford witnessed a terrible tragedy when three members of the Home Guard were killed whilst practising on Hednesford Hills.

The Hednesford Home Guard met on the Monday evening to be shown their latest weapons – two grenade launching rifles. These were SMLE Mark 111 rifles which had been modified to fire grenades. A cup holding the grenade was fitted to the muzzle which itself was strengthened by copper wire. Captain Pearce had been appointed as their bombing and weapons instructor, being a veteran of World War One. He was ably assisted by Councillor William Morris who had also served in that war. They would demonstrate the new acquisitions.

To fire the rifles the man had to almost lie down with feet foremost and the grenade was then fitted to the cup by a comrade. Having successfully explained and demonstrated the rifle, Colonel Pearce split the men into two groups. By 8.35 p.m. some twenty men from each group had fired the launcher, leaving twelve from each group to have their turn. At 8.40 p.m. Lieutenant Bond moved into position whilst William Morris assisted. Suddenly there was a terrific explosion and a disaster had happened. Bodies lay everywhere and it was difficult to know who exactly was injured. Fortunately there were some twenty or more qualified first aiders in the group who did what they could for the injured.

With as little delay as possible ambulances from nearby collieries arrived along with five local doctors, two nurses and the police. The seriously injured were ferried to Wolverhampton Hospital, sixteen being taken in total. On admission it was found that Corporal John Borton was already dead while William Morris, who seemed at first to have only suffered a fractured arm, died on July 1st. The third man to die was seventeen year old Kenneth Blastock who had suffered multiple injuries. He died on July 2nd. The remaining thirteen eventually recovered.

65. The grave of Lieutenant W. Morris.

All three were buried in St. Peter's Churchyard the following weekend and were given headstones similar to those killed at the Front.

The eventual outcome of the subsequent inquest was "Accidental Death" and the coroner concluded that the accident was in no way the fault of the rifle, but possibly caused by a faulty grenade or to it being fitted wrongly to the cup.

Historical note – Military historians have since commented that the supposed ingenious device added to the rifle was "even more dangerous" than the hand thrown grenades and was "dangerous in the hands of inexperienced men". Apparently the copper wire used to strengthen the muzzle frequently became loose after much firing.

December It was announced that Rawnsley School was to close due to subsidence and the junior pupils would transfer to the new Hazel Slade School which had opened in Cannock Wood Street on April 27th, 1931. ★The seniors had already gone to Littleworth. The official closure took place on February 14th, 1943.

1943

July Hednesford Clinic and Library was officially opened up at 11a Cannock Road on July 28th. The library was above the clinic and was one room 32ft by 22ft, accessed by a staircase. The clinic had an assembly hall, minor ailments room, waiting and undressing rooms and a doctor's room. On the first floor were a dentist's room, staff office, recovery room and bath room. The front of the building had been practically rebuilt and the old garage and outbuildings were used as a shelter for perambulators (prams).

66. Site of the old clinic and library on Station Road.

At the opening Councillor Hampton, talking of the delay in getting the new facilities, said, "The difficulty in Hednesford had been securing a site. Full advantage had not been taken of the old facilities already provided.

As many children under one year old died in Hednesford in 1902 as died in the whole area in 1939, despite the big increase in population. But the present progress in health was due entirely to the improved medical services."

★We have to remember that people still had to pay for medical attention.

1944

Hednesford cinemas changed hands. Mr. Williams, who had been in the area since 1914, sold them to Messrs. Griffiths and Cockburn of Walsall.

August The Council were to ask the Government for 200 prefabs after the War "to give favourable consideration to members of the forces applying for housing after the War". Our area had some 3,000 men in the forces and about 1,000 had been married during the War or would be married immediately after.

November The Home Guard was to stand down and a parade was to take place on Sunday December 3rd.

1945

June A tragic accident happened at Hednesford Cadets night at the Drill Hall when fifteen year old Basil Clansey of Booth Street was shot and killed. ★More of this incident can be found in *More Murder and Mayhem around the Chase* by your author.

67. Empire Cinema.

July It was announced that Hednesford would get a Civic Hall. The idea was first muted in February, 1938 and plans had been drawn up the following year, but the War had interrupted those. The idea was to have a gymnasium and swimming pool at the end of the building and a concert room and many other facilities next door. By 1939 a site had been earmarked in Anglesey Street and a grant had been offered. However, that grant "was not now forthcoming and a high percentage of the cost would have to be found in Hednesford". It was suggested that an application should be made to the Ministry of Education for a grant towards the final cost.

1946

March A competition was held to choose a name for the development in Cannock Wood Street in Hazel Slade of a small village of prefabricated bungalows. Each home would have a large scullery with cooker and refrigerator and plenty of cupboard space, a living room with coal fire, two bedrooms with central heating, a W.C. and bathroom. There were to be 52 new houses of which 36 had already been completed by February with 8 more partially erected and 3 covered externally and roofed. Over 100 people participated in the competition and

"Spring Valley" was the proposed new name. It was chosen because it would be a "little village springing up in the valley at Hazel Slade". The 10s prize was awarded to Mr. R. Cox of Rawnsley Road.

May/June Hednesford Accident Home – A cheque for £323 10s, money which was raised by holding a dance and having collecting boxes, was presented to the Home to wipe out all the debts incurred during the War. Repairs were needed as were extra nurses, but it was made clear that the Home's future could be taken over by the Government. Colonel Peake, Chairman of the Committee, added, "We are rapidly approaching a new era with regard to hospital services and ultimately it would seem that voluntary subscriptions will be replaced by compulsory contributions under the control of a national unifying authority. In such a scheme as that this Accident Home will be a very small constituent and just where it will fit, or whether it will fit at all, is a matter of speculation."

Historical note – In July 90 year old **John Thomas Ward** of 414 Belt Road gave his memories of the area to the *Cannock Advertiser*. Born in Halesowen he came to Cannock Wood when just a child and remembered there were no roads at the time, just grass covered lanes looked after by an overseer. In nearby Beaudesert Hall the Marquis took a keen interest in the village, paying half the Sunday School fee of two pence per child providing the money saved by the parents was spent on clothes for the children.

Other memories were of the sad death of Mr. Eskrett's daughter by drowning in 1869 in Hednesford Pool (Eskrett had kept the Anglesey Hotel); the 1873 Army Manoeuvres which meant the building of Hednesford Railway Bridge in 1874; and the opening of several new pubs, including the Red Moor and the Uxbridge Arms.

August Known to all the older residents of the area as "Jack the Mail Man" **J. Foster** of 7 Hill Top, Hednesford was born at Sandon in 1876. The whole family survived very well on just fourteen shillings a week, their diet consisting of healthy food like beef, bacon, home-made bread and farmhouse cheese. When interviewed he said that despite his hard life he had never had a day's illness in his life and at seventy he still worked all day on his small farm.

As a lad he had to walk three miles each day to school and when he arrived home he was expected to work in the family garden. At eleven he began to work on a local farm at fifty shillings per year with food provided. His hours were from five in the morning until six or seven in the evening. In the summer months the hours were even longer. He then took to driving the mail horse- drawn van round the area, including rounds from Eccleshall to Stone, Stone to Stafford and Cannock to Hednesford. Those journeys were at night, from eight o'clock in the evening until five in the morning. In the winter it meant that horses often slipped on the frosty roads and fell, causing much panic and wild behaviour. "The wilder they were the better I liked them," he said. He would buy only "nappers and bouncers" costing from fifty shillings to seven guineas. The best horse he ever had cost just £4 and another good one came from German gypsies. He said that his love of animals still continued and he had cows, pigs and poultry in the field at the rear of his home.

September Accurate Screw Thread Limited of Victoria Street was selected to send a model of an electric iron to the "Britain Can Make It Exhibition" as its product was considered to be "amongst the best in Britain". The factory also made the prototype of the turbine blades used in the jet aircraft which had just broken the world speed record.

Historical note – The name was derived from the fact that the company was the holder of patents for the making of thread rollings, dies and machines for the accurate screw threads on metals. For a time Mr. Harold Morris, the managing director, was employed by Rolls Royce and introduced the use of accurate rolled threads into certain important aero-engine parts. In 1945 the company acquired the factory in Victoria Street on the site of Mr. Taylor's old corn stores. Consisting of four main departments for turning, milling and drilling and a tool room it had the most up-to-date equipment.

Machinery for the production of metal boxes, electrical fittings and jet turbines and aero engines were made and with the rearmament programme under way there was increased activity in the making of jigs, tools and fixtures. The firm also did lots of work for the Admiralty, especially with the construction of the two-stroke petrol engine. Another principal product was hydraulic-pneumatic riveting equipment for use with "pop" rivets used for aircraft, omnibuses, coach bodies and metal fabricated houses. The factory would last until the late 1960's when it closed. In 1969 the factory site was taken over by Automatic Transmissions.

October Sunday Observance – A public meeting expressed the wish that Sunday films should be allowed to continue. The Council agreed by 30 votes to 23. The War had certainly changed opinions!

November Proposed provision of a bus station on the Anglesey lawn area, costing £938 for scheme one and £1776 for the second which would have a rest room. Buses travelling from the railway bridge into Hednesford would turn right and stand in positions in front of the Anglesey Hotel. A 22 ft. carriageway would be provided for motor cars and part of the site would be reserved for public conveniences and a rest room to be built later. (The latter were never to happen.)

68. Bus station in Market Street.

Historical note – Older residents of Hednesford may well remember the Number 7 bus to Cannock via Pye Green being stationed there as well as the No.1 to Cannock via Chadsmoor and the No. 8 to Rawnsley.

December Hednesford factory closed down. Messrs. Joseph Lucas Ltd. of Birmingham had started a small factory in Belt Road in 1942 and later had moved opposite to the Old Soldiers Institute in Anglesey Street where they made parts for tanks. In the early days at Belt Road they made 500 components per week which gradually increased to 15,000 at the Anglesey No. 1 factory. They then moved to Anglesey No. 2 site in the Anglesey yard. Mr. Warren was the first manager. Because the War had ended they moved back to the Kings Street Works in Birmingham. They were to return later to take over the factory once owned by Moore's.

Historical note – Chaseside Industries Limited (the Enamel Works).

Founded by Messrs. Frederick and Norman Male in 1946 in what used to be the Red House racing stables in East Cannock Road, the brothers had previously owned Regent Casting Company in Hednesford. Starting alone by 1950 they had eventually trained and employed over sixty people, including a few women. Their work was principally enamelling castings sent to them by other manufacturers with baths as their speciality. Then they specialised in the vitreous enamelling of domestic equipment like cookers and stoves.

They then came up with the idea of making baths out of light weight materials as the cost of transporting heavy enamelled iron baths to the furthest corners of the world, where new housing projects were underway, was expensive. For twelve months they experimented with fibre glass and other materials before producing their first bath which was produced entirely at their factory. It was so successful that they expanded into mini baths, sink units and seats for office use. Orders were eventually exported to places like Trinidad, Singapore, New Zealand, Mauritius and Rhodesia as well as Scotland and Ireland. The beauty of the product was that they could be "nested together" cutting costs.

Each bath took just four hours to make and while the resin was drying in the hot air oven, which they designed themselves, they could continue to make others. Four layers of resin and fibre glass went into each bath making them as strong as any metal ones. (A

69. Enamel Works with B. Allen and D. Male.

fourteen stone man demonstrated the strength by jumping up and down in one.) They were believed to be the first of their kind anywhere in the world. They were easy to clean and could not chip or rust like enamelled metal ones and they also, it was claimed, kept bath water hotter because fibre glass was a very good insulator. Eventually they made the bath side panels.

In **December, 1966** the firm was taken over by Century Enamel Limited when Chaseside Industries went into liquidation. The new firm produced cast iron hollowware for the building industry as well as the gas and room heating industries. It also produced fancy goods and hardware.

1947

February A new church hall opened at Pye Green. The land was given by Lord Hatherton who had given land previously to build Pye Green Mission.

March The 1947 Winter – The first snowfalls had happened on January 24/26th and on February 2/4th and again on February 8/9th. Each fall was progressively worse than the previous one, but by Saturday February 15th most roads had been cleared. However, heavy blizzards began on the evening of March 4th and by the morning hundreds of households had to dig themselves out, snow having penetrated through roofs and under doors. Winds, which sometimes reached gale force, blew the fine snow into drifts, some reaching as high as twelve feet. The district was almost isolated with roads completely blocked. The blizzard continued through Wednesday with hardly a respite, the wind being particularly fierce in the afternoon.

The trains between Rugeley and Hednesford were badly affected because of drifts and a bus on its way from Hednesford to Littleton Colliery was caught in a drift and completely buried by Wednesday. Three coaches on their way to a Darlaston factory with girls from Cannock and Hednesford got stranded on Watling Street. By the Thursday the trains were still having difficulty in getting past Hednesford and had to turn round and go back to Walsall. Tractors were in great demand for the delivery of essentials items like vegetables and milk.

70. Christine Gregory (nee Baker) in the 1947 snow on Church Hill.

Ask anyone who lived through that winter and they will all have tales to tell. I vaguely remember walking from the common at the top of Heath Street where we lived through a pathway surrounded by mountains of snow. It had taken dad and the three neighbours a day to dig.

June The Council decided to invest in new aluminium houses and began compulsory purchases of various pieces of land – in Cannock Wood Street, Hazel Slade opposite the newly built prefabricated bungalows; in Eskrett Street; View Street; and Bradbury Lane. By November the Council had almost two thousand requests from local builders to erect them. It had to cut its figure to 300 due to national demand, but by that month 15 had already been built in Hazel Slade.

July The names of those who fell in World War Two were to be added to the War Memorial. The Ministry suggested that the cost could not be properly met by the War Memories Powers Act of 1923 and so it was thought that locals would "desire to subscribe individually and voluntarily" for the purpose. The local councils and British Legion were to help with the public appeal for funds. The tablet was finally added in September, 1949.

1948

April Hednesford Accident Home – At the end of 1947 its assets were £1,623 2s 1d, but liabilities were outstanding for repairs and decoration. Captain Peake, who had been Chairman for 15 years, stated, "We are still unaware of the precise use to which the Home

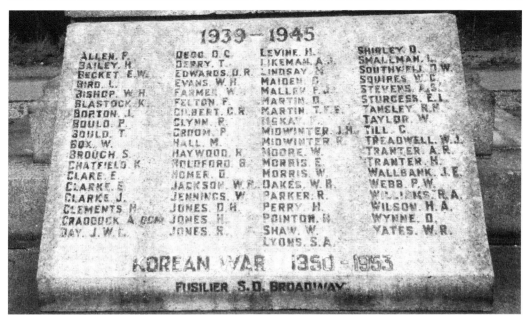

71. War Memorial's 1939-1945 tablet.

will be put after July when the new Health Act comes into operation, but we have the satisfaction in knowing that the buildings are in good condition and that there is a favourable bank balance". Unfortunately the number of in-patients had decreased owing to better safety conditions in the mines, but that meant lower income. He also stated that Miss Blakemore had been in charge as matron for some 41 years. However, he had to resign due to leaving the district.

June It was proposed to have a Sports Stadium for Hednesford on the site of the old reservoir. A Walsall firm of architects, acting for Mr. Claude Thomas Roe, had asked the Council's permission and it had been granted. The plans were for a first class sports centre covering such sports as cycling, motor cycling and car racing, foot running (athletics today), roller skating and other sports. Until more permanent buildings could be erected it was proposed to have temporary, portable ones. Mr. Roe had already purchased land on the south side of the Hills and north side of the Accident Home to use for car parking and had submitted plans for four conveniences to be placed around the perimeter. Refreshments would be provided from a mobile canteen.

Historical note – The reservoir had closed in 1930 when it became defunct owing to housing estates being built at higher levels. A new site at Gentleshaw had been obtained.

July Further plans were announced for the Hednesford area, including more houses for Bradbury Lane (there were already 16 new three bed roomed houses and 6 two bed roomed ones). At Pye Green four aged persons bungalows were to be built and more houses for agricultural workers. Tenders were also in for 24 houses in Mount Side Street and permission had been granted for 20 aged persons bungalows in Eskrett Street.

For transport in the area there would be a daily bus service between Hednesford and Heath Hayes via Littleworth Road and Wimblebury and the buses on the Rawnsley service should now include Hazel Slade. As for Hednesford Railway plans had been submitted by the Company to improve the booking office "sometime in the future".

November Hednesford Railway Station was again the subject of many complaints with local women's organisations calling it "inconvenient, uncomfortable and shabby". L.M.S. had completed plans to make alterations before the War, but they had been put on hold.

November On Sunday November 14th a new plaque was added to the Wimblebury War Memorial commemorating those who died in World War Two. The parade, headed by the Hednesford Salvation Army Band, met at the Trafalgar Inn and marched to St. Paul's Church where the crowd was so large that not everyone could fit into it. Rev. Lafford and Mr. Richards conducted the service.

December The Postmaster General declared that Hednesford telephone service would be improved. At the time it was a branch office under the control of the head Postmaster at Walsall. However, owing to the shortage of equipment, plans for a new automatic telephone exchange could not be carried out for a few years, but it would be transferred from its present premises to the post office where new equipment had been installed.

1949

January Hednesford was to get its new British Restaurant and Hall costing nearly £20,000. The committee asked the architects to include offices and arrange the steel framework in such a way that further buildings could be added in the future to include a stage for plays. *The only public hall that Hednesford had had in the past was the Public Rooms on Rugeley Road built in 1876. It had become "The Empire Picture Palace" in 1912.

September The Council approved plans for a new Bus Station in Victoria Street and a compulsory purchase order for the land was recommended.

December By this time the West Cannock No. 3 Pit had closed. Opened in 1871 it stood at the southern end of the valley opposite Queen Street and Platt Street.

72. West Cannock No. 3 Pit.

The Fifties
(1950 - 1959)

1950

August Miss Annie Blakemore announced her decision to retire in the October as matron at the Accident Home after 43 years of service. Originally from Wheaton Aston she was trained at Queen's Hospital, Birmingham and was on the staff as a private nurse before being appointed a sister there. She became matron at the Accident Home on January 1st, 1907. She well remembered a water main bursting in May, 1908 in the field close to the Home which washed down the garden wall and left six feet of soil in the drive. Sadder memories included the pit disasters at Wimblebury and West Cannock No. 5's where miners lost their lives. She intended to move back to Wheaton Aston on retiring. Annie Blakemore died on February 24th, 1952 aged 86.

★From 1951 the hospital would be used as a general practitioners hospital for local doctors with a consultant service as required by Wolverhampton and Stafford Hospitals. By November, 1952 it had had improvements to the ward, sluices and bathrooms at a cost of £729 12s. It had a new kitchen range and complete interior and exterior decoration. There were new bedside lockers and a radio service to the ward. The average occupancy had been raised from two to seven.

73. Accident Home c.1950.

October The Joseph Lucas Factory opened in Market Street on October 3rd on the old Moore's site and by April, 1951 it employed 130 with 20 of them men who were engineers, toolsetters and supervisors. The manager was Mr. C. Handley. The building was comprised of a machinery shop, a winding shop and assembly shop. The factory serviced replacements for switches and made car accessories including trafficators (lights) and magnetos.

*During the War it had been used as a storage area by the Ministry of Food.

November The Council decided to stop plans for a possible open air swimming pool in Hednesford Park. The original idea had been for a boating lake, but fears of mining subsidence halted the plans – "although there were no plans for workings in the area of the Park in the next five years coal seams could still be worked there".

December The Marquis of Anglesey sold many freehold properties and ground rents the family had held realising nearly £53,000. There were 88 lots for sale, including ground rents for two cinemas and shops in Hednesford along with the Drill Hall and Accident Home and almost the entire village of Hazel Slade. Some of the sales were as follows:-

Mr. Follows of Rowley Park, Stafford paid £1,150 for the ground rents of the Drill Hall, Mines Rescue Station, N.C.B. garage, Gas Works, the public mortuary and houses in Victoria Street. He paid £6,500 for the ground rents of 85 houses in Bradbury Lane, Rugeley Road and Brindley Heath leased by the West Cannock Colliery Company. As well as those he also got Stafford House, the cottage stables and stores for another £1,500. He also paid £600 for the rents of 21 houses on Church Hill as well as the working men's club; while at Hazel Slade he paid £4,500 for the rents of 140 houses, shops and a hotel.

The Empire Cinema ground rent went to a Birmingham firm of solicitors for £1,500 while the ground rents for 16 houses and four shops in Stafford Lane and Cannock Road, High Town went to Mr. Bailey for £650. Mr. King of Birmingham paid £5,400 for the rents of nine shops in Market Street and house printing works and the working men's club in Eskrett Street.

1951

April Hednesford's New Civic Restaurant opened. Equipped with all the latest kitchen apparatus and utensils it could cater for 700 people between 12 noon and 2 o'clock. The large hall was electrically heated and had fluorescent lighting and underneath the mat covered floor was a polished surface suitable for dancing. At one end was a raised platform to serve for public speaking or a band.

74. Civic Restaurant c.1954.

Two licenses to sell alcohol at the venue were refused after observations from the police. A bar had been allowed at the very first dance, but it had been in one of the designated cloakrooms and that had caused congestion in the other, resulting in coats and owners being difficult to organise. It had taken until one o'clock for everyone to get away. The police also said that there had been some 14 year olds at the dance. By February, 1952 the restaurant, which had been labelled a "white elephant" by some, was paying contributions to the rates. Even the Market Hall restaurant was taking £30 per day.

September During another rain storm the Froysel Cottages on Rugeley Road flooded. It was to be a regular occurrence until they were finally demolished sometime in the late 1960's early 1970's. (Locals often nicknamed them the "Hope Cottages" in the hope that they didn't flood.)

75. Rugeley Road flood c.1970. Notice the partially demolished Froysel's cottages.

1952

January Hednesford Railway Bridge – Again in the limelight the Council asked for an estimate for providing a footbridge over the line with an idea of asking the Government for the money. Mrs. Hotchkiss said that anyone who had ever been to it would know that it was dangerous and she hoped "the County Council would accept a tender for a footbridge to be approved". Mr Jarvis said it was a real danger and "only recently a woman walking on the footpath had had her handbag wrenched off her arm by a passing car".

By **December, 1954** the County surveyor had agreed that a footbridge was desirable, but having regard to other bridges on County roads which were even nastier "it would be extremely difficult to give Hednesford Bridge priority". He had seen the railway company and had submitted a scheme for 11 yards of tubular steel fencing, costing £50, to be erected. In **May, 1955** the Council heard that the Government had turned down their request for funding, deciding that it was not proved to be an accident spot. Mr. Bailey commented, "It seems people have to die before the importance of removing the danger spot is realised." How often have we heard that!

May Hednesford's Market Hall – Woolworth's had expressed an interest in having a new store at Hednesford and the Council approved plans for alterations and extensions to the Market Hall. The new building would contain a stock room, staff dining room, lavatories, kitchen and a small office. The new "uni-seco" building would be semi-permanent and have a ten year life approval. Unfortunately the old hall could not be demolished as it was still in private hands.

1953

June Coronation Celebrations – Instead of large parades the area split into many street parties of which the following are just an example. Unfortunately on some of the chosen days poor weather interrupted some events.

Upper Mount Street – On Coronation day 78 children were taken on a coach ride to see the decorations in larger towns. After there was tea provided in Mrs. Craddock's field in Bradbury Lane followed by sports and the children were given a memento of the occasion. Just round the corner in Mount Side Street a party was held for 25 old residents and 48 children. Each child received a crown money box while the old people had the cup, saucer and plate.

76. Mount Side Street party. L-R back row - A. Lewis, J. Williams, Mrs. Pickerill and M. Street. Front row - Mr. Street, Mr. Craddock, Mr. and Mrs. Jukes, Mrs. Prince ? and Mr. Pritchard.

Bradbury Lane Estate – People of Howard Crescent, Shaftsbury Drive started with a fancy dress parade followed by tea for the children. Each child was given a cup, saucer and plate as a souvenir. Later there were sports events.

Rawnsley – The celebrations began with a fancy dress parade followed by tea for the first sitting of 200 children. Sports then took place on Rawnsley football field during the late afternoon and evening. Each child up to 15 was given a cup, saucer and plate. On the Saturday the old folks were treated to tea in the Church Hall.

Brindley Heath – In conjunction with the R.A.F. Station sports were organised for all the children (some 400 of them) and bags of sandwiches were given to each child. After tea they went to a film show in the hangers.

Littleworth and Church Hill – A fancy dress parade was followed by tea and sports. Despite the poor weather the event finished with a bonfire.

Pye Green – Tea was given to approximately 100 children in St. Mark's hut because of the bad weather and each child received a present. Prizes were also given to the winners of various races.

July All the residents of Brindley Village were to be rehoused on the Brindley Heath Estate. Representatives of Brindley Heath Parish Council, with Mr. S.G. Clare as its chairman, were told that talks between the National Coal Board and Lichfield Rural Council had ended with agreement to build 92 houses instead of the 60 first suggested. There would be four bedroomed houses as well as three and two bedroomed ones along with bungalows for the elderly. It was also agreed that the Rural Council would take over the 30 houses situated on Brindley Heath Road and renovate them, with a bathroom and toilets added. By June 1956 10 houses were being occupied in Bracken Close and 14 more almost ready.

August The first part of Hednesford's New Bus station in Victoria Street was ready to be used. The road into the station, including an unloading bay and two loading bays which would take two buses, had been completed. It was decided to begin to use it as soon as possible and also restrict the use of Anglesey Crescent as a bus station as much as possible.

The complete station was finally ready in August, 1955 and had seven platforms, five for the Walsall Corporation buses, one for the Green Bus Service and one for Midland Red. Eight buses could use it at one time with others waiting in an adjoining vehicle park. Some shelters had been provided and more could be added if necessary. The next idea was to make up Victoria Street so that buses departing for Rugeley could go round Victoria Street on to Rugeley Road without having to go through the town. The only buses to use Anglesey Crescent would be those on route from Cannock to Rawnsley via Huntington Terrace (the No. 8).

1954

May Hednesford Park was to be enlarged with the acquisition of more land so that further facilities for local sports clubs could be added. That land along the Rugeley Road had originally been allotments opposite Froysel's Cottages. Next to that land was the Polish Club begun after the war.

July The Council expressed the wish that the R.A.F. Station should be permanent as it had become part of the community. Events two years later would possibly change their minds!

August Hednesford Reservoir site had been bought by Mr. Claude Roe in 1947. He proposed to terrace the slopes with space enough for seating for a possible 60,000 people (100,000 standing). Along with Mr. Les Marshall, the Birmingham speedway promoter, they planned to bring speedway to Hednesford. Mr. Roe saw the possibilities of the site after visiting America where he witnessed stock car and midget car racing, but he was held up by "red tape". However, the first stock car meeting was held on August 29th. A special safety fence was erected, consisting of steel rails, steel hawsers and concrete. A shale track of approximately a quarter of a mile in length was installed.

During the winter of 1954 he planned to add more permanent shelters and covered stands and in the spring of 1955 a tarmac race track about half a mile in length, containing two hairpins and a steeply banked section, would be built. During the following summer he hoped that he could attract Formula 3 car racing, motor cycle racing, speedway, stock car and hydroplanes as well as show jumping and trotting, boxing, dancing, roller skating, a children's playground, and a drive-in cinema.

Fully aware of the potential of the plans the Council were delighted with his plans and agreed to allow the partners to use adjoining land as a car park to accommodate up to 25,000 cars.

1955

January The Civic Restaurant – With reference to the dances the Council banned "Saturday night bopping". The manager, Mr. G. Gridley, said it was unfair "to those attending the dance for the enjoyment of an evening's ballroom dancing" and "for every person who indulges in bopping it takes up the space of three people". So far as he was concerned only 30 out of 300 present were boppers. However, bopping would be allowed on Tuesdays as the

74. Civic Restaurant c.1954.

dance was only attended by the young. He added, "When people got to the age of 20 and over they thought bopping a bit silly." He also said there was an objection to "creeping" as it blocked the centre of the room.

April The Hednesford area would get automatic electric lighting for all streets. Hednesford's first electric lights had been installed in July, 1923, but only parts of the area.

June Some of the houses in Abbey Street and Blewitt Street were to be demolished as they were unfit for habitation.

1956

February The revised tender of £4,214 for the construction of the footbridge over the railway was recommended for acceptance and the contractors were requested to carry out the work as soon as possible. Hurrah, at last! The same sentiment appeared in the following letter:-

> "Seems to be it was troubling someone's conscience half a century ago!
> But let not the local residents think nothing has been done to improve the bridge
> in the last 50 years. Why, quite recently electric lamps stands have been erected
> on the pavements to show pedestrians how much room they haven't got. In the
> meantime I suggest Station Bridge be called "The Bridge of Sighs" or should that
> be "Undersize"?"

★ That letter was from Eddie Martin of 20 West Hill Avenue and dated March 17th.

By **May** permission to proceed had been granted and contractors were on the job on what was "probably one of the longest delayed improvements in the country". Twenty five years before Hednesford Traders Association had agitated for something to be done, followed by the Chamber of Commerce. The outbreak of World War two was blamed for delays.

February Hednesford Post Office was to close in future on Sundays. Previously it had opened from 9 a.m. until 10.30 a.m. The main reason for opening had been telegrams, but "with the growth of the telephone service and the provision of telephone kiosks" that was no longer deemed necessary. Similar patterns may develop today with the growth of the internet and texting.

April Rawnsley School was finally demolished.

October R.A.F. Station was to close due to Government cuts. Work on the Camp had begun in November, 1938 and about 100 men were employed. It was finally opened in the autumn of

78. R.A.F. Station 1950's.

79. R.A.F. Station 1950's.

1939. It had three churches and was the only recruitment camp in the country to have a Jewish Synagogue and so all Jewish recruits were sent there. It had over 81,000 regular and national service recruits pass through its gates. It was estimated that 150,000 had been stationed there. During the War it was known as No 6 School of Technical Training and at the end of the War it became a personnel dispatch centre. The School of Recruit Training opened in October, 1951 and nearly 10,000 airmen at the Camp gained their swimming certificates and 1,650 their marksman's pass. Its voluntary band gave over 1,000 performances round the country.

The last passing out parade was on **Monday December 3rd.**

However, the Camp was not to close just then as the crisis in Hungary brought thousands of refugees to England and many were to end up at the Hednesford Camp. By **December 13th** some 700 refugees were expected to arrive at Rugeley Trent Valley Station on route to the Camp, transferred from London. With agreement from the Home Office Hednesford Camp would be used as a reception centre for them, but it had not been decided whether the Camp would be a permanent home or just a transit camp. The refugees were to include families and single people. The R.A.F. was to remain at the Camp for the time being and act as a catering service.

Typical of the generosity of the area some refugees were invited out to local houses for the Christmas and volunteers went to the Camp to hand out gifts, though that was frowned on by the British Council for Aid to Refugees as "gifts needed to be evenly distributed". However, pocket money was given out which was used in the local shops and churches, mainly Our Lady of Lourdes as most of the refugees were Catholic.

The Camp was finally to be put up for auction on **April 7/9th, 1959**. At the end of that month the County Council proposed to acquire the area for youth purposes with playing fields for Hednesford and Rugeley youth clubs, together with three huts for changing room facilities and a caretaker to be appointed. It also recommended that a portion of the land would be used for weekend camps with two huts for storage.

December Hednesford Stadium site was put up for sale. Mr. Roe, who had converted the site into one for stock car racing, wanted to sell it. He suggested it would be an ideal caravan site.

He had been annoyed that the Council had built a Sports Stadium of its own in 1950 when he had proposed to make his site into one. By **April, 1958** he had been refused permission to sell it as a proposed caravan site.

1957

January It was decided that the Camp would be a transit one only. There had been some suggestion that as many as 500 Hungarian refugees would like to work in the local mines as they did not want charity (the Polish men did so in World War Two), but that idea proved controversial. By July there were "definite signs that the miners of Cannock Chase were going to adhere to their previous resolution not to agree to the Hungarians being allowed to work in local pits". A ballot at Hilton Main Pit defeated the proposal to allow them to work by 567 to 167. The reasons given by the miners for their stance were the fear of local unemployment in the future, the language difficulties and they were annoyed at not being consulted from the start.

May East Cannock Pit closed. Situated down East Cannock Road the company was founded in 1870, but ran into difficulties. Finally a second company began drawing coal in 1881.

July Hednesford was to get a new Police Station built in Anglesey Street to replace the one in Cannock Road which had been built in the 1870's. It was completed in 1959, but by 1969 it was decided to convert it into a hostel to house 18 young officers. There would still be a police presence for the public in the building, but for how long? ★The old station on Cannock Road is still there and is a block of flats.

80 Old Police Station.

1958

June The Toc H Organisation was to get new rooms in what had been three stables at the rear of the Anglesey Hotel. They would have a meeting room and kitchen.

Historical note – The brainchild of Reverend Philip Clayton he sent his senior chaplain, Neville

Talbot, to France to set up a rest home for men fighting at the Front. It was to be an alternative to the brothels behind the lines frequented by many troops. Talbot got a hop merchant's house in Poperinge, Belgium and began the rest house on December 11th, 1915, which contained a library, rest area and a chapel in the attic. It was soon nicknamed Talbot House and later became known as Toc H after the radio signallers' code.

At the end of the War a house, known as Mark 1, was set up in Knightsbridge, London in 1919 and men who had used the original began to use that. Soon there were three houses in London and when the members left they set up their own Marks in their home towns. The intention then was not only to encourage comradeship but to do service in their local areas. Hednesford's Toc H began in the 1920's.

81. Anglesey Hotel c.1905.

August Hednesford was to get a new library. The old one in Cannock Road in what used to be part of a pawn shop was deemed "unsuitably housed and wrongly sited" which had led to a decrease in adult usage, but strangely an increase in junior use.

December By this time West Cannock No.1 had closed. Started in 1869 opposite Green Heath Road it was one of the oldest mines in the area.

1959

Historical note – Hednesford 70 years ago. The following are memories of **Cliff Craddock:–**

Mr. Thomas Arnold was chief engineer at the West Cannock Colliery when their offices were like three bungalows on the Cannock Road. Across the road was Lee's Farm and a little further down Cannock Road Mr. Tranter kept a butcher's shop. On the opposite side was a tailor's shop where one could get a suit for 10s; a hard hat for 2d; and a pair of socks for 3d. You could also get a type of spring collar for your shirt for just 1d. At Pointon's shop you could buy a quarter of sweets for a penny and half a pound for just one and a half pence. Across the road the Police Station had two constables and a sergeant.

He also remembered a Mrs. Broom, a baker, who took bread out in a three wheeled basket truck and at the Rising Sun, High Town the landlord was Mr. Burgoyne after whom the street was named. It stood on the corner of Cannock Road and that street. Various "characters" he remembered were Half Soaked Dick, Harry Archer, old lady Grice who kept "The Lump" (the Plough and Harrow), Old Tuppence and Sidney Sharp who carried parcels. Bagnell's Coffee Shop was a popular rendezvous. The first motor car he saw in Hednesford was in 1908 at the wedding of Mr. & Mrs. Bates of 249 Station Road.

Comments from **Mrs. Balfour (nee Miss Lyle Bagnell)**, who had not been in Hednesford for 43 years, which said that she was "surprised at the way Hednesford had deteriorated since she had last been there" and "surely someone with some initiative and money could start up some business to liven things up" brought sharp criticism from the traders. They said that the town had "a bright future and were very optimistic". One trader did blame the Council adding, "If Hednesford is a shoddy place the Council are to blame as pavements and roads haven't been renewed for years. Whenever there is a heavy downpour the water stays in front of several of the shops. Whilst Cannock has undergone a thorough change Hednesford hasn't altered much over the past twenty years. It has had a new footpath over the bridge, a civic restaurant and a bus station and that is all." I think we still hear those same complaints today!

February Brindley Heath Station was to close as the Camp no longer existed. It had opened on August 26th, 1939 to serve the Camp on the Chase.

March Civic Hall? Twenty years had elapsed since it was first muted. The site had been chosen in Anglesey Street about 100 yards past the Tivoli Cinema on the opposite side and provisional plans had been drawn up. Hednesford had been promised £3,000 from the National Fitness Committee and another £1,000 from the Ministry of Transport and Social Services, but the War had intervened. The military occupied the site which had been a temporary centre and "requisitioned" stocks of materials belonging to the women members. The committee laboured on, but gradually interest in the scheme dwindled. Finally the site was lost when the new Police Station was built there.

The Sixties
(1960 - 1969)

1960

January The area suffered a serious subsidence when cavities opened up on Church Hill, creating a hole 34 foot in length and 15 foot wide in the road and on the footpath. At its deepest point one hole was 6 foot and fences of nearby houses sank some 2 feet into the ground. Underground pipes were twisted and broken and "according to local opinion it was the worst subsidence ever". South Staffs Waterworks Company spent a day filling in the cavity and making the area safe. ★It would not be the last subsidence in that area.

April The future of Hednesford Railway Station was discussed. The old station would disappear and a new one be built below the bridge. It was stated that "the planning of the new permanent station would be carried out as part of the electrification programme expected to affect the line in 1962. The design of the new station and platform layout would depend on the track remodelling, finally agreed upon for railway operation purposes." There would still be a bridge carrying the road and traffic over the line and the road and footpaths could be widened subject to finances. If it was practicable the new station frontage would include a service way to allow cars and other traffic setting down or picking up passengers to draw clear of the highway.

82. Railway bridge c.1905.

The old booking office on the bridge was closed later in the year and was eventually demolished.

June Albert Street off Church Hill had two rows of terraced houses separated by "a rough and badly rutted track". When it rained rubble was swept down on to Church Hill and "money spent on cleaning out the drains would have surfaced the street many times over". Residents complained to the Council about the poor condition of the road, calling it "the forgotten road". They said, "The neglect is due to the Council refusing to improve it. Whenever there is heavy rain the soil is washed away and deeper holes appear in the ground. The soil has been washed away to such an extent that the sewer grids are now nearly two foot above the normal ground level. Jagged rocks jut from the ground and huge gaps have appeared." They claimed that the road was used fairly regularly by tradesmen and visitors to the nearby churchyard of St. Peter's.

74 year old Mr. Turner of 44 Albert Street said he had lived there for 70 years and in that time nothing had been done to improve conditions. Mr. Griffiths of No. 48 said that 30 years ago the Council had taken measurements and put up signs and it looked as though their troubles were over, but after 6 weeks those signs were taken down and nothing more was heard from the Council. All the tenants agreed that "if the road was at Cannock it would be renovated immediately, but as in other things Hednesford is only a secondary concern". The Council said they could do nothing about it as it was an "unadopted road".

*Unadopted roads are those which the Council has not taken on the responsibility to keep maintained. One such road recently was the upper section of Keys Park Road leading to Wimblebury.

*It may surprise readers, but even as late as the 1970's not all roads had tarmac surfaces even though houses had been there for years. Wider ownership of cars would change that, but not completely (see part of Simcox Road leading to Albert Street on Church Hill for one example).

83. Simcox Street c.1950.

1961

April Fafnir Bearings at Littleworth – The factory first opened in 1941 when it was Fischer Bearings, a subsidiary of Timken. The Company had some 1,400 men at Littleworth and Wolverhampton and they made bearings for cars, aeroplanes, conveyors and domestic appliances.

The men worked in two shifts, night and day, thus keeping the factory working at all times, especially during the war. No external structural alterations were allowed during the war as it was considered that the natural surroundings, which included considerable stacks of tiles, provided a most satisfactory camouflage against enemy bombers. In 1960 Fafnir Bearings, an American owned company, took over and asked for permission to build an additional block which would employ a further 60 men. In **April, 1962** the new factory section opened to replace the "shadow" factory erected in the early days of the war.

In **August, 1974** the company announced an expansion of the factory which would virtually double the work force by the following spring. It would occupy 90,000 square feet and be ready for **April, 1975**. In **September, 1974** they held an open day for the public to view the new plans.

June Did you know that we once had a small Railway Museum at Hednesford? It was situated at the Chase Works between Station Road and the railway and employed three men and there the restoration of historic rolling stock took place. At that time it had a Maryport and Carlisle Railway 6 wheel full third coach built in 1875 under reconstruction. I am not sure if the public was allowed to visit, unlike the Chase Railway today. The wagon works in Hednesford had been set up in 1877 and most of it was situated between the Cannock Road and the railway.

84. Wagon Works.

1962

In **December, 1961** Meadway Spares Ltd. had applied to the Council for a proposed lease of the stadium on Hednesford Hills for ten years with an option for further time to have all types of motor and motorcycle sports. In return the Company was prepared to build and develop the site into a sports venue. They proposed to build two tracks in the bowl, one of which would be sunk three feet with a safety barrier. They also wanted to lease adjacent land for a car park.

In **January, 1962** the Council agreed to let the stadium, but only on the condition that no events took place on Sundays. Some councillors argued that they "must have regard for those who valued the peace and quiet of the Hills on one day a week" adding, "The Council must have regard to the value of the Sabbath even if people were not going to church in such large numbers". One Hednesford Councillor added, "Would the Council consider this sort of thing on Shoal Hill?"

By **February** Mr. W.J. Morris of Meadway Spares agreed not to promote Sunday events, but stated that it was "absolutely essential that club functions would have to be in operation on Sundays to be able to run the stadium economically" and that might include final testing of machines. However, he did agree not to promote Sunday events for the public. In March the Council voted against allowing any Sunday sport, but were "prepared to negotiate on a broad basis for the use of the site on a Sunday". Later that year the first stock car racing took place.

January Littleworth Girls' and Littleworth Boys' Schools amalgamated and became Kingsmead Secondary Modern School.

February Wimblebury, "A Ghost Village coming back to life" – The need had been great to rebuild Wimblebury owing to its derelict state. Mining subsidence had played havoc with the houses, but the Council was determined to rebuild. The first new roads were laid in 1936, but the War had intervened. The slum clearance had been almost finished by 1959. The new Wimblebury would boast 106 houses with 35 garages and two shops with accommodation.

85. Arthur Street numbers 27/57 c.1950.

By **April** tree planting to beautify the area had taken place on Kennel Mount which was a former pit mound. It was hoped that the Parks Department would look after the site. By May the Council was ready for tenders for the first 100 new houses and the opportunity would be given to those "who had been driven away to return to their native village if they wished". It was hoped that a self-contained community would soon develop.

86. John Street numbers 72/82 c. 1950.

Interviewed in 1964 older residents remembered the old place. 73 year old Jack Barratt said, "They all seemed sociable with each other, but if an outsider came it often used to end in a bit of a "brodgel". He described it as being "a bit of a wild west town" often with fights, but everyone drank in the pub later. Harry Halworth said, "The village was a very notorious place in those days. At one time no one would ever pass through Wimblebury if they could avoid it."

★Your author remembers stories being told of local football teams who played against Wimblebury sides being told to make a "speedy" exit after the match, especially if they won!

April By this time Wimblebury Pit had ceased to draw coal after its connection with West Cannock No. 5. The shafts were filled in and the site eventually cleared.

In **July, 1963** Wimblebury Methodist Church opened and was one of the first buildings in the new Wimblebury. The land on which it stood had been donated by Mrs. Gladys Clarke of 39 Piggott Street in memory of her late husband.

April The new German Cemetery near Broadhurst Green was started and would have 4,800 graves from the two worlds wars. The first part of construction was finished in May.

June The Council were to build around 250 more houses for the miners in the Hednesford area – a possible 90 in Bradbury Lane; 34 in Mount Street; 162 on Rawnsley Road; and 42 in Eskrett Street.

87. Piggott Street numbers 2/8 c.1950.

August It was announced that Hednesford was to get a multiplex store. Woolworth's had bought the Market Hall at a sale held at the Royal Oak, Cannock on Monday, August 21st for £17,500. It was too early for them to give exact details, but it was thought that they might demolish the old market and build a new store. The firm had been satisfied that "Hednesford was a thriving area". By **February, 1965** Woolworth's said that it was "not very high on their priorities list", but it could happen "as soon as circumstances would permit". Hednesford residents complained that the site was by then a "terrible eyesore and was spoiling the town" and was a "big blank patch in the town centre which looked very dull". The development never happened, but eventually the market was replaced by new smaller shops still there today.

88. Market Hall.

October 13th Hednesford Canal finally closed after just over one hundred years of use. Built by the Birmingham Navigation Company in the late 1850's as an extension of the Wyrley and Essington Canal it had a thriving boatman and family community in the nineteenth century. However, with the growth of the railways it gradually began to decline until it was no longer economically viable.

89. Hednesford canal.

1963

It was the year for change in Hednesford, not all for the good!

February Blagg's bought the Empire Cinema site. It had closed a few years before in 1957 and had been used temporarily as a spiritualist church. Also the Tivoli had closed in January, 1963 and was awaiting demolition and a new market was to be built in its place. Hednesford would be left without a cinema. The Council purchased the Tivoli site and the building would be adapted as a market.

March Under Beeching's plan the Chase Railway line would close for all passenger traffic.

May Hednesford's Hospital to close – It was not fully occupied and the building was "old and badly affected by mining subsidence". It was deemed that the costs to repair it would be too great. Originally it had been run by the Cannock Chase Coalowners Association and then the Ministry took it over, but it rarely had many patients. It was decided that it should stay open until treatment was available at the proposed new clinic and out patients department at Cannock.

July There was a proposal to allow Stock Car Racing on the Hills on a Sunday in August and September between the hours of 3 p.m. and 5.15 p.m. as an experiment. It caused uproar at the Council meeting. When the matter was discussed again in November Mr. Morris said that he had carried out a survey of 100 residents near the site about Sunday racing and "no fewer than 95% supported it wholeheartedly". He said that he thought that the original rejection was based on "chaotic traffic conditions, inadequate parking and staffing which existed in 1954", but those drawbacks had been eliminated. Once again the matter was deferred.

90. Stock Car racing c.1963.

August St. Peter's Churchyard was to be levelled as well as the churchyard extension. Most of the gravestones had already been moved. The new churchyard opened in June, 1964.

1964

The rail closure for passengers would take place on April 4th unless objections were received by March 2nd. The "Paddy" train from Cannock Wood Pit to Bates' Corner had already stopped on January 31st. The closure was finally announced in **February, 1965**.

March It was announced that Hednesford's oldest Methodist Church, Bethesda on Station Road, was to close in April – "Gradually the congregation had decreased and it was financially very hard to keep going". It would amalgamate with St. John's further along the road.

April 16th. Hednesford's new library, begun in 1963, finally opened.

Historical note – In the early years it began with a collection of books in the Sunday School of the Hednesford Wesleyan Methodists. In 1925 the Public Library Act was passed and on May 18th a library was opened at St. John's Institute. At the same time it served as an employment exchange. Later the library moved to Cannock Road. Plans for a combined library, clinic and fire station at Hednesford were put on hold because of the War.

91. Bethesda Chapel.

1965

June The "Ghost Line" as it was called was to open for a special day trip out organised by Stanton's Bakery for the benefit of its 600 employees. The Station Master, Mr. J.C. Forrest, said,

92. Outing to Blackpool.

"If a party organiser can get 400 or over, or even 300, and made the arrangements trains could be put on if available".

At the same time it was announced that the "Rail Axe" could hit Hednesford again and British Rail might close the goods depot at the station. The main freight to Hednesford was flour for the local bakery. Most other goods were already being collected from Walsall. Twenty six people worked at Hednesford Station, though not all connected with the goods yard.

By **April, 1966** the goods operation had moved to Stafford, but the yard was still as busy. The station master was still responsible for the wagon repairs along with West Cannock No. 5 and Cannock Wood Collieries and still had 24 men employed. However, the station only dealt with small packages carried by the goods trains.

June In **June, 1964** the mid-week market on a Tuesday had closed due to lack of patronage. Its temporary site was in Victoria Street, but a permanent place was being looked at on the Tivoli site because that was being demolished. However, it would not be made available until market trade picked up. In **November** the Council announced that the market would move to the Tivoli site. However, in **April, 1967** the market was still in Victoria Street and "continues to decline in numbers and popularity". 8 out of 10 lock-ups were used just once a week on a Saturday and only 2 out of 10 open stalls were being used. The income to the Council was just £9 per week.

93. Victoria Street Market.

In **January, 1968** it was finally announced that the market would move to the old Tivoli site after the Council had purchased the former goods yard and adjoining properties. The new site would be let for three years. The new market was finally opened on Friday, **December 12th, 1969.** It had cost £11,000 to purchase the land and a further £5,000 to build the permanent site in Anglesey Street. It would open every Friday and Saturday.

94. New market site.

August George Street on Church Hill – Residents, like those of Albert Street, complained of grass and weeds growing from the kerbstones and new buildings were set up "amidst grass and weeds". They also complained of the crossroads at the top which "were a hazard" as there were no signs indicating a school (St. Peter's Junior).

1966

January A new housing estate was being built at Splash Lane with around 250 new houses. The first phase was to be ready in February/March with 26 houses and three shops would follow later.

January Hednesford was to get a new telephone exchange in Eskrett Street with 800 lines to replace the manual one which had 500 lines. It had started its life at Printcraft Press in Market Street and then in 1948 had moved to the Post Office. Once the new exchange was running it would only need one person to operate it.

February Hednesford Raceway – A new grandstand was being built which would hold 1,000 spectators. The "figure of eight" and "destruction derby" events had been introduced in 1965. On **August 7th** the Council allowed the first ever Sunday meeting as a trial for just two meetings.

The raceway finally began to make a profit in the early 1970's. It had made a loss on every meeting for the first three and a half years, but the company "stuck at it". Another first for it was the staging of "It's A Knock Out" in **May, 1972.**

95. *Hednesford Raceway.*

March West Cannock Farm, Bradbury Lane – Unusual you might think to include a farm, but it had become a timber business. Before World War One it had been a mixed farm of about 30 acres owned by the Dunford family. However, the War altered all that and they turned their hands to haulage, conveying war materials by horse to the R.A.F. Camp and later loads of heather to be used as packing for goods. In the 1920's they collected and delivered timber, still by horse. In the 1930's they introduced steam tractors to move the timber and with timber under the Government control the business became profitable. In 1942 Mrs. Dunford died, but her husband continued the business employing some 30 men. The business was affected by a slump in home timber sales and so between 1952 and 1955 they decided to enter the tree and root clearing trade.

By 1961 the business was in the hands of Ian Dunford and he had a fleet of vehicles, including mobile cranes and transporters with a workforce of ten men. They then turned their attention to the planting and care of trees (tree surgery), planting around 40,000 per year and cultivating some 170 acres of land.

April The demolition of the old Hazel Slade village began. All Saints Church had been closed in 1961 and was finally demolished in 1966. 26 new homes were to be built in Hazel Slade, mainly in Albert Street, to replace the terraced houses. One councillor said, "We owe it to Hazel Slade and particularly the people living in atrocious conditions at present to move on these 26 dwellings and treat this as a special case." Lots of the village had already been demolished and was being rebuilt, but as could be expected those left did not really want to move. By December, with most of the place demolished, the residents of the 26 houses preferred to stay saying they "did not want to leave their old haunts". They preferred to "brave the winter" rather than take up alternative accommodation. Mr. & Mrs. Albert Brace of 8 Chapel Street said they "now looked out on to open space where another row of terraced houses once stood", but they preferred to stay as his job was at nearby Cannock Wood Pit. His wife, Alice, was born in the village and he had moved there in 1922.

96. Demolition of Hazel Slade.

97. Albert Street with All Saints at the top.

Historical note – The first mention of Hazel Slade that I found was around 1744 when the Ingramthorp family had a racing stable there. The Paget family also had several coney warrens there in the 1770's and in 1776 the Old Park Colliery was set up and lasted for some forty years until 1816. In 1864 the Cannock and Rugeley Colliery Company opened up the Wood Pit and by 1867 the miners' village was started with 144 houses, shops and bake houses and in 1876 the Hazel Slade public house opened with Thomas Davis as landlord.

By 1878 the streets were lit by gas and water (not for drinking) arrived for the houses in 1880. The old Park workings had closed, but were soon followed by the opening of Cannock Wood Pit by the Cannock and Rugeley Colliery Company.

Talking of his memories of Hazel Slade in the 1890's seventy nine year old **J.T. Pugh** said that he had worked at one of the five communal bake houses, owned by Mr. D. Alldritt, and had

98. Hazel Slade Inn.

helped in pan greasing, dough mixing and the baking. At his bake house there were two ovens which were coal fired and bread cost 4p to 5p for a 4 pound loaf. He also remembered the village had no gas or electricity, just paraffin lamps and candles. There were just five water taps in the village and when they froze in the winter people had to wait for the water carts or try to get water from the little spring down past the "brickshed" as they called it at the back of the racing stable.

In 1904 approval was given by Lichfield Council to lay gas mains to the houses and in the same year the village got its first official sewerage works. By 1910 the homes finally got drinking water and flush toilet facilities. In 1934 electricity arrived in the village and in the same year Cannock Urban Council took over the running of the village from Lichfield Rural Council. The demolition of the old village was complete by 1968 and some new houses had already been built. In 1971 the foundations of the new village were laid in Cannock Wood Street and on June 8th 1973 Cannock Wood Pit closed.

August 19th/20th After a prolonged heatwave our area suffered a torrential storm which began on the Friday evening and lasted almost all of the Saturday. Parts of Hednesford were flooded, especially Hednesford Park which once again became a lake, reminiscent of the nineteenth century.

99. Hednesford Park flood - L-R S. Oakley, G. Bore, L. Rowley and C. Richards.

November Hednesford had a new Health Clinic in Eskrett Street which replaced the old one in Cannock Road. It was announced that finally Hednesford had risen from being a "black spot" in infant mortality to below the national average. It had had a death rate of 63.5 per 1,000 compared with the national average of 50. It now boasted a rate just under the national rate of 19 per thousand.

1967

January The Council announced plans for the "Future of Hednesford" mainly due to the increase of cars. The planners were "emphatic that to achieve any kind of success for the town traffic must be excluded from Market Street". They suggested that cars should be diverted from the railway bridge into Victoria Street and there should be service roads to supply the shops. There would be four main car parks, one at each corner of the shopping area with a multi-storey one built on the disused railway land near the station. They also envisaged a youth centre and technical college in the immediate vicinity. To give an idea of the problem with cars the planners published the following:-

1965 population 8,000 with some 1,280 cars; 1971 population 10,300 with some 2,060 cars; 1981 population 17,050 with some 5,627 cars. I wonder what today's figures are with lots of families owning more than one car?

The solution came in 1968 when it was decided, with the agreement of the Hednesford Traders Association, to make Market Street a one way system.

August Members of the Salvation Army had raised £1,700 to build a new hall, but the Council said that a bye law prevented the building of a new hall unless car parking space was provided for one in six who used the building. It was decided to redevelop the old hall. By **March, 1973** the 90 year old hall had been refurbished and had a new kitchen, electric heating and florescent lighting.

100. Market Street. Mr. John Gray is on the extreme right.

Historical note – The Salvation Army Corps 256 arrived in Hednesford in the early 1880's and on Sunday March 19th, 1882 held their first service in the Market Hall which they had taken for the twelve months. Thousands turned out for the occasion and Hednesford was packed from the Hall to the Railway Station. Having purchased land on West Hill (on the corner of today's West Hill and West Hill Avenue) General

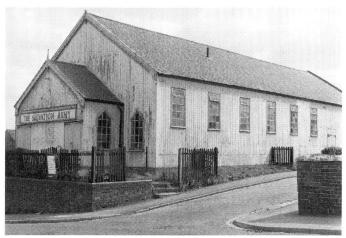

101. Salvation Army Hall.

Booth arrived on Monday January 26th, 1885 to lay one of the four memorial stones. As he said in his address the building would be of the cheapest material with a wooden structure and stone foundations and the plainest possible. It would be 90 feet long, 40 feet wide and 20 feet high and cost around £600. With a raised platform at one end it should hold around 1,000 people. Mr. Hale of Netherton had the contract and laid another of the stones. "Captain" Farmer of Hednesford had the honour of laying a third while Major Corbridge of Sheffield laid the fourth. After the ceremony they retired to the Market Hall for a tea meeting - the Hednesford Band, led by bandmaster Mr. Poole, guided the way. (Older residents of Hednesford will well remember being entertained by the band and its songsters on numerous occasions as well as their regular visits to local public houses collecting.)

102. Salvation Army songsters.

In November 1988 the Corps moved from its old wooden hall to new premises - the former Technical College's canteen and gymnasium in Anglesey Street - and the official opening was in March, 1992.

Incidentally Booth Street, opposite the Hall, got its name from William Booth, founder of the Salvation Army Movement.

*These last two entries about Market Street and Salvation Army show just how dominant the motor car was becoming in our lives! Strangely your author has never had one.

1968

February When the Anglesey Hotel was rewired over the Christmas period rumours began to spread that it was to be demolished. It had no preservation order on it at the time, but was later to become a listed building. Supposedly it was to become a site with shops and a new licensed premises. The brewery denied all rumours saying they were only going to modernise the inside.

At the same time the Drill Hall was sold to Mr. John Hills of Brownhills for £9,000. He dealt in crane hire and demolition work. On **May 1st, 1969** it reopened as a Bingo Hall and had cost £4,000 in renovation. That would last until late **2011** when the redevelopment of Victoria Street took place to build the new shopping area.

April Further subsidence in the area – Two families had to be moved out of Rawnsley homes on the new estate after cracks appeared in their garage pathways. A slope of about 4 inches appeared in some rooms. In February, 1969 cracks began to appear in Wimblebury's Methodist Church which had only been built six years previously.

August The land once occupied by Wimblebury Colliery which had closed some ten years before was to be given a new lease of life with the building of a precast concrete factory. It was to be the first phase of building by Concrete Midlands Limited, costing £75,000 and would initially employ 20 people which could expand to 500 if it was a success.

October However, on a more sombre note it was announced that 100 men were to be made redundant from Hednesford Engineering Limited in Victoria Street and it would close later on. The factory had been there since 1960 and was a subsidiary of Boulton-Paul Aircraft Company of Wolverhampton, a member of the Dowty Group.

1969

March Work on a pedestrian footpath which was to be installed in Stafford Lane next to the road/rail bridge had begun. It was almost the same design as that over the line at the Station Road/Bradbury Lane junction. The work was completed by April.

August "Slum" clearance reached its peak with about 1,500 houses having been declared "unfit for habitation". In the next two years some 700 would be demolished including houses in George Street, on Church Hill, in Booth Street, Forge Street and McGhie Street. Most of those were 100 years old and had no damp course, just solid floors. They only had cold running water and the toilet facilities were in the back yard separate to the houses. The longest road they had to tackle was Bradbury Lane.

103. Pedestrian bridge, Stafford Lane.

The Seventies
(1970 - 1979)

1970

January Bates' Bridge on the Rugeley Road was becoming a danger spot, both for pedestrians and drivers. There was no real footpath under the bridge, just a tiny, narrow walkway no more than a foot wide on the Bestmore side only. In the previous five years there had been 66 accidents reported to the police, but there had probably been many more that went unreported. An Action Committee was set up to resolve the problem. It came up with three possibilities – traffic lights; a traffic island; or a new road cut through the railway embankment. British Rail had quoted £41,000 to have the bridge widened. The committee also drew up a petition to send to the Ministry of Transport.

104. Bate's Bridge.

1971

January The Civic Hall in Hednesford was undergoing refurbishment which had started in **December, 1970** with the restaurant having room for some 300 diners and carpeted throughout. A local competition was held to rename it and "The Aquarius" was chosen. It was reopened in the **April** and "hurried plans were being made to extend the cellar after the bar staff discovered it could not hold enough beer". With the serving of alcohol it was planned to "keep undesirables

105. The Aquarius.

away" and women dancers were told not to wear stiletto heels so as not to damage the dance floor. "Free heel rubbers" would be issued. In keeping with the new policy the wearing of denims was banned in the **August** and would last until the October. It was thought that only the "rowdy element wore denims". There would also be a ban on under–18 year olds.

By **March, 1972** ballroom dancing replaced the pop groups on a Saturday night and the so called "boot boys" had their disco on a Thursday. Prices were 30d for bands and 10d for the disco.

February There was to be a new car park on the corner of Rugeley Road and Victoria Street, access being gained via Cardigan Place which at the time was "unmade" and full of potholes.

March The East Cannock Colliery had closed in 1957 and the site had been bulldozed. The Council had "allocated the site for industrial, public and open space with allotments and woodland", but they were asked to allow it to become a warehouse development. Having already submitted plans to the Ministry they rejected the new idea as it would prejudice any of their own proposals. If there was to be any industry it would only be on 25% of the site. By **August, 1976** 50 acres of the site, bordering Stafford Lane and East Cannock Road, was being developed. The company, Multigate Properties Limited, were to construct around 400 private homes, leaving about a third of the site for public open space. Eventually that site would become the Stagborough Estate with grassland bordering the East Cannock Road. By **August, 1977** work had started on the houses, but Multigate had sold their stake in the venture and no one seemed to know who the new owners were.

June Traders in Hednesford ignored possible fines for displaying their goods on the footpath. Some retaliated by saying it "had been going on since the end of World War One" and did no harm. Other traders said, "Showing goods outside was vital to trade"; while Herbert Rollins declared, "We take up just twelve inches of pavement". Today those goods seem to have been replaced by delivery vans using the pavements as parking spaces!

August The Council set aside £10,000 for a clean–up plan for derelict land in the Hednesford area, particularly the old West Cannock Colliery site in Pye Green Valley, owned by the National Coal Board. It was decided to clear the area and then do something with it, but what? It took another thirty years or more to decide to finally build houses on it having landscaped it. In **January, 1975** the Council purchased the 110 acres of the old pit sites in Pye Green Valley with a view to new housing. It was also decided to have a further extension to Blake School. In **May, 1976** they purchased the remainder of Pye Green Valley from the National Coal Board with ideas to use it as an area for housing, schools and public open space. The reclamation, which would include culverting the brook, was expected to take about three years. So far, as I write, it has its famous "road to nowhere", but some houses have now been built.

September 14th On that Tuesday afternoon the warehouse at the rear of Peake's shop in Hednesford caught fire. With the fear that it might spread and the possibility of explosions shop assistants from Peake's and other local shops and passersby dragged furniture away from the blaze. Mr. Arthur Peake was injured during that exercise. Four fire engines attended the blaze and brought it under control within an hour. The front of the warehouse which faced Rugeley Road was damaged and plate glass windows in nearby shops were cracked. Four cars were rescued from Blagg's car park almost behind the store and only slightly damaged.

October Bestmore Tool Works on Rugeley Road was taken over by C & J Hampton Limited makers of "Record" tools. They hoped to expand and develop the business. They were confident that the leading brand names "Bestmore" and "Snail" would add to their own range of tools which they exported to over 120 countries.

November Blake Boys Secondary School was to get a new extension costing around £400,000. It had opened in **September, 1964,** originally as an all boys school with the girls still at the High Town Girls Secondary School on Belt Road. In **September, 1972,** after the extension was complete, the two senior halves of the schools were amalgamated with Mr. George Harris as the headmaster; the lower school (first and second year pupils) went to the High Town School. In **May, 1983** the Council suggested selling off the High Town School and bringing together the upper and lower halves as there were better facilities at the Blake School.

1972

February A company in Jersey, Fifteen Two Limited, who owned the old Market Hall in Hednesford, put forward a plan to redevelop the site which had stood empty for ten years. They wanted to demolish the building and replace it with four shops and said that if other shops became available they would consider taking them over as they thought "Hednesford was a worthwhile area for development and investment". Those shops would be the first in the town for nearly four years. That block of shops still stands today opposite the town clock.

The demolition of the Market Hall was complete by May to make way for two of the shops. Mr. Close, the architect, said, "A lot of leases on older property in Hednesford are due to expire shortly and many people feel this development (the two shops) could start the ball rolling for a lot more rebuilding of the town."

106. Market Street Crescent.

July Hednesford Ex-Servicemen's Club held its 50th anniversary. Formed in 1922 they first met in a schoolroom opposite the present site. It began as a meeting place for soldiers from the War and, despite having no beer, had 52 members. The first building, opened in 1923, was a wooden hut costing £75 on the site of the present concert room. The land was rented from the Marquis of Anglesey for just 1s per annum. It also had a bowling green. The committee then loaned £500 from the British United Services to construct the present building and secure the land. They later repaid that loan and from 1950 onwards saw a gradual growth in membership. In 1963 the committee room and games room were added.

August Property Company W. A. Blackburn Limited bought a big section of Market Street between Eskrett Street and Lloyd's Bank and several properties in Eskrett Street with the intention at least of rebuilding nine of the shops in Market Street.

November The Council planned to demolish the prefabricated bungalows at Pye Green along Plantation Road, Tower Road, Spruce Road and Broadhurst Green as soon as possible.

107. Prefabs, Pye Green.

1973

February The Council began a massive rebuilding in Hednesford with 74 new houses in McGhie Street, 56 in Littleworth Road, 28 at Wimblebury and 4 in Foster Avenue. The prefab sites at Hazel Slade and Pye Green would also be developed. In **May, 1974** they announced further plans to build more houses – 18 in Abbey Street, 44 in McGhie Street and 60 in Platt Street.

April It was announced that the notorious bridge at Bates' Corner might not come down that summer when the National Coal Board stopped using it as no less than five authorities had to agree, including Lichfield. By **November** it was decided that it might have to remain as it could be used to transport sand and gravel. The idea of traffic lights was quashed, despite an accident happening only the week previously when three people had to be taken to hospital. In **December** it was suggested that the sand and gravel could go by conveyor rather than rail, but British Rail refused.

June Part of the old Hednesford Brickworks site was discussed as a possible area for a new refuse tip. Objections came from the Hednesford Ratepayers Association. However, it went ahead. In **February, 1974** a new row broke out because "rubbish was not being covered every night" as promised and was causing smells. Also the supposed fencing around the site was inadequate. The local residents claimed, "Hednesford was being used as a doormat".

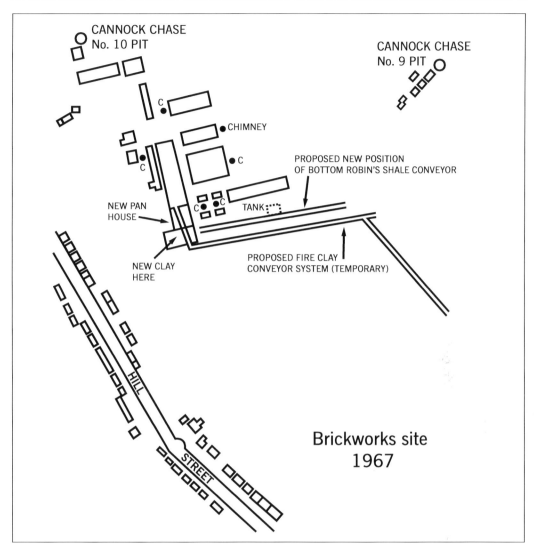

CANNOCK CHASE
No. 10 PIT

CANNOCK CHASE
No. 9 PIT

C

CHIMNEY

C

PROPOSED NEW POSITION
OF BOTTOM ROBIN'S SHALE CONVEYOR

NEW PAN
HOUSE

C ● C TANK

NEW CLAY
HERE

PROPOSED FIRE CLAY
CONVEYOR SYSTEM (TEMPORARY)

HILL
STREET

Brickworks site
1967

108. Map of Brickworks 1967.

November Kingsmead School (the old Littleworth School) had new extensions opened. They included a sports hall, craft room and science laboratories.

1974

January Five Oaks Investments of Birmingham put plans before the Council to build 70 new "mini houses" on the Rugeley Road opposite the park where the Froysels houses stood. One councillor amusingly said,

109. Littleworth School c.1950.

"They certainly live up to their name of miniature properties. I would suggest they need a midget population to inhabit them."

April The redevelopment of Hednesford Town Centre under the guidance of Blackburn Development of Leamington Spa was well under way. Mr. Derek Davis, letting agent for the developers, said that almost all the units had been taken. Work had started on the demolition of the old shops and when the new ones were built they would have offices above the shops and a car park at the rear for about 100 cars. The car park actually holds 30/40 cars.

110. Market Street 2006.

1975

February Hednesford Hills Raceway – Again the possibility of a car park was raised. It was decided that the owners should build it and provide for extra security for pedestrians. As to the road leading up to the site the owners had to ensure that cars stayed on the road provided which included going over the ramps; some had gone round them forcing pedestrians to jump out of the way. The Council also confirmed to the owners that the actual site of the Raceway was not part of the land given over to the people of Hednesford by the Marquis of Anglesey in 1933.

April Bates' Bridge – Despite many protests the bridge was to remain. British Rail said that it was "still classed as operational" and Blue Circle Aggregates Limited might want to use it from their base in Rugeley to transport goods. The Council also said to get the suggested island or traffic lights the land at the corner of Station Road and Rugeley Road would have to be compulsory purchased.

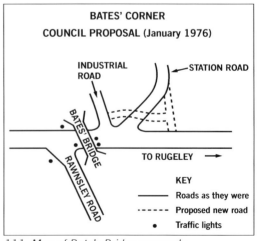

111. Map of Bate's Bridge proposals.

May The Council's scheme for 80 new houses in Hazel Slade (the Garden Village Estate) was well under way despite the bad winter. Maxim Construction Limited had forecast that the whole estate would be finished after twenty months. However, the West Bromwich firm went into liquidation and by the **October** were in dispute with the Council. Residents complained of "streets without lights and rubbish strewn amenities infested with rats" as well as "two years of mess".

At Rawnsley the picture was no better with the new 56 housing estate having ground to a halt with only half complete, while in Littleworth Road only 28 bungalows had been completed.

1976

January Hurricane Night – The ferocious winds caused a great deal of damage in the area with over 6,000 trees being flattened on the Chase. St. Peter's Church had tiles ripped from its roof and masonry blown down the aisle. A stained glass window above the altar was smashed and a new, especially equipped holiday caravan for haemophiliacs was wrecked causing over £400 worth of damage. Unfortunately it had not been fittingly insured. An off-license in Rugeley Road had its chimney and television aerial crash through the roof, while at Wimblebury a bus shelter collapsed like a pack of cards.

January After a five year campaign could the Bates' Bridge question be solved? Work seemed to be underway on a £136,000 scheme to install traffic lights. However, residents nearby still were not happy as they wanted the bridge to be knocked down. In **February** British Rail again refused to sell the bridge to the Council, despite Blue Circle saying they were no longer interested in using the line. Still hoping British Rail might change its mind the Council delayed its plans for lights.

April Fafnir Bearings – Bad news for the area as the American Company, part of the Textron Group, announced that they would sack about 70 workers. The men had been on work sharing for months. In **May, 1978** the Company announced that a further 600 jobs could go and redundancies were already in the pipeline. Plans for a four day week were called off, but 200 jobs could be lost. The fall in work was blamed on market depression. Its sister factory in Wolverhampton was also at risk. In July Mr. V. King, the Personnel Director, announced that there would only be 70 redundancies. In response the workers went on strike in **September.**

August The second natural disaster in the year hit the Chase when large areas set fire because of the unusually hot and dry summer. For days firemen worked around the clock fighting nearly a hundred outbreaks. Forestry workers helped and the Milk Marketing Board sent tankers to transport thousands of gallons of water. Bowmakers factory also lent earthmovers to dig "firebreaks" to slow down the spread of the fire. Fortunately a very wet Bank Holiday Weekend helped to put an end to the flames and only about 300 trees were lost. Ironically in the **September** violent storms caused flooding throughout the area.

1977

March In an article headed "Decaying Face of Hednesford" local traders complained about the "crumbling brickwork, broken tiles, derelict buildings and strewn rubbish" around the town making it look like a "Wild West shanty town". They were not talking about "some dingy out of the way back street", but Market Street. Private landlords were blamed for neglecting their properties. Councillor John Desmonde said, "It was a job to let shops and one was still empty." He added, "In Hednesford there are about eight semi-derelict properties, three of which might have to be demolished if owners would not improve them." While Alec White said, "When we have derelict properties like we have, what chance is there of getting the town back on its feet?"

However, despite all that the Hednesford Traders planned to celebrate the Queen's Jubilee. There would be a music festival, maypole dancing, a pram race round the town, sports' days at the various schools and an "It's a Knock Out Competition". The event would finish off with a Festival Ball at the Aquarius.

In **May** the state of Hednesford's Market Street had been brought before the Council. Councillor Len Jackson said, "The Council has got to do something because a total redevelopment of Hednesford is needed. It should never have been allowed to deteriorate to the state it is now." The Council replied adding that they planned to redevelop it and those plans should be ready within three months. Alec White, Chairman of Hednesford Traders, said, "Hednesford had become a ghost town when a lot of homes in surrounding streets had been demolished, but at last the Council is replacing them and new people are moving in." Another councillor sarcastically added, "Show Prince Charles Hednesford when he visits Cannock in July for the Jubilee celebrations."

In **October** the Council announced a short term scheme to tidy up Hednesford's "eyesores". A mid-term solution was to cut out through traffic and Market Street was to be confined to shopping with a small scale development of the shops. In the long term Market Street would become fully pedestrianised.

1978

January Plans were announced to widen the road at the awkward Market Street and Station Road junction and also part of Station Road itself. The Council owned almost all the properties, except Pointon's Sweet Shop. He objected to selling it as he was born there and the office was his mother's living room. In **September** Pointon's shop was reprieved as the scheme was proving too expensive.

February To keep the pressure on the Council about the state of Hednesford local newspapers were only too glad to print letters. One such was from eleven year old Robert Matthews who wrote, "At the Beehive Corner there were shops, now just stones, bricks and litter. There is a row of houses along Station Road that are boarded up with grass high and hedges overgrown. One shop in Market Street has dirty posters in the window and has been up for sale for years."

In **March** the Hednesford Traders Association met to discuss the problem. They were in favour of a restricted access to Market Street rather than a full pedestrianisation scheme. In June the Manpower Services Commission approved a clean-up scheme.

February Bates' Bridge – Chase road safety watchdogs claimed that the bridge was "falling down". They asked the Council to press British Rail into demolishing it as soon as possible, but the Council blamed B.R. for not setting a date. Finally B.R. said that the top deck of the bridge was to be removed later that year, leaving the pillars standing. However, people still complained because the eastern column had no footpath at all and it severely limited visibility for pedestrians crossing from Rawnsley Road. On **Sunday, March 19th** British Rail workmen removed the top of the bridge, but there was still no agreement on the pillars.

April Hopes were dashed for the reopening of the rail line. British Rail said that passengers would have to bear the full cost even though the line had never really closed as it had been used for freight.

May Chase planners approved plans for 20,000 square feet of industrial and warehouse space next to Chaseside Industrial Estate in Lower Road. It was applied for by Clevecolne Limited which wanted two single storey blocks of six-self contained units. The local residents wanted houses or shops on the site.

August Stafford Lane's bridge over the railway was to be repaired because of fears that it might crumble. The work was to take two weeks.

August A strike at Stanton's Bakery was called off. Workers had claimed that the management were undermanning the shifts; supposed to be an 18 man shift, but as few as 12 at times. The bakery had become part of Allied Bakeries, a nationwide concern. In **March, 1979** over 50 drivers were to lose their jobs and the bakery would only deliver to Wright's confectionary shops and their own outlets. The bulk of the deliveries were being taken over by Allied branches in Wombourne and Wednesbury.

112. Stanton's vans.

★Quite separate to those issues there was a national bread strike in **November**. Do readers remember the queues outside Tenants in Hednesford and their policy, quite rightly, to serve only people who had used their shop in the past?

October The Co-op wanted a new superstore for Hednesford in the town centre, preferably on the site of the old Tivoli. At the same time a building company (unknown) had unveiled plans for a quarter of a million scheme to reshape entertainment in the town. Plans included a squash court, motel, restaurant and bingo hall.

1979

April Fears were raised over the safety of school children walking over the Stafford Lane bridge as there was no footpath. A proposed infants' school at High Town would mean more children using the bridge. The original idea, put forward by British Rail, was to build a tunnel under the railway, but that proved too costly. A scheme had been suggested for a footpath on the south side to be constructed during the 1980/81 programme of spending.

May Hednesford's outdoor market would move to the car park behind the present site in Anglesey Street, owing to the plans for the new Co-op.

May The campaign for improvements to Hednesford continued. In 1978 ex Army Major, Arthur Smart, had proposed that jobless teenagers should be used to clean up the area from Rugeley Road to the Aquarius, especially the land behind the shops. Arthur Smart was the company secretary for Automatic Transmissions in Victoria Street. Unfortunately he had died since making the suggestion, but Councillor Alcock took up the campaign. The group were trying to establish exactly who owned "the waste land" at the back of Market Street. They also wanted early action on the Beehive Corner site which they said "needs to be landscaped and the corner widened so that buses and lorries do not put pedestrians at risk".

June Fafnir Bearings – It was announced that the factory was to finally close at the end of the year. Some 530 workers and 70 office staff would lose their jobs. In **September** it was announced that another American firm, part of the Dana Organisation, was trying to buy the Company. It could mean some jobs could be saved, but 400 had already been made redundant. However, in **November** it was announced that the takeover would not happen because of a national engineering dispute.

The Eighties
(1980 - 1989)

1980

February Pye Green Valley – The Council announced a plan for the redevelopment of the area with up to 800 houses, a primary school, shops and a public house as well as open space to be on the site. At least 65 acres were for new houses and 35 acres for educational use. It was hoped to begin the scheme by the end of 1981. When the far end of the site was complete it contained Pye Green Valley Junior School, the Samson Blewitt public house, shops and houses. The remainder of the valley is now being developed.

March/May Hednesford Hills – Residents claimed that it was being used as a tip with the Coal Board tipping waste there as well as the litter from the Raceway. A petition of over a thousand signatures called for the total ban on cars at all times. Mr. Morris, who ran the Raceway, hit back saying his venture was "a valuable employment and commercial asset to Hednesford". (His lease renewal for the stadium was due in another eighteen months.)

The residents also blamed the Council and the police for their lack of action over prosecuting anyone for the littering. The Council retaliated by blaming the people of Hednesford for dumping rubbish.

October Rawnsley and Hazel Slade were to become the sites of a jobs boom with two developments. The first was industrial units on the site of the old Cannock Wood Pit and the second units off Littleworth Road (Cannock Wood Industrial Estate and Anglesey Business Park respectively). Meanwhile in Hednesford itself Kwik Save announced a new store in the town on the site of empty shops; the new Co-op was about to open; Tennants would have a new building; and the Post Office refurbishment was almost ready. Things looked like they were on the up for the area.

December 5th The Co-op opened its new store in Anglesey Street, Hednesford, adjacent to the small market and large car park. Mr. Bangham, president of the Society, in his opening address said the Society had been disappointed when they had had to pull out of Hednesford, but

*113. Opening of the Co-op Store - Mr. C. Bangham, Robertson's Golly, Sue Bott and L. Irons in the foreground of photograph left. * The Golly would never be allowed today!*

had done so for two reasons. Firstly their previous store was too small and secondly Hednesford's town shopping centre seemed to be dying. However, they were glad to be back with "this large new store". Miss Sue Bott became the new manageress.

1981

February Plans for a traffic free Market Street were again under discussion. Yellow lines had been introduced, but people delivering to shops largely ignored them. Again there were two options – a one way system or complete pedestrianisation.

May Because of the furore over Hednesford Hills the Council's plans for the site were put on show. They included tree planting, space for a car park and defined walkways. In **November, 1983** volunteers planted tree saplings on the Hills. Conservation volunteers had fenced off and prepared the site for oak, beech and pine saplings supplied by the Council.

★Once quite a feature of the area between 1900 and 1920, but thankfully rarely experienced since, 1981 saw three large fires in various properties. In April the Double M Club in Glover Street, Wimblebury was gutted. While later that year Hednesford's motor bike shop, Kaston Kawasaki, also set fire causing £100,000 of damage to new bikes in the store room. In December, during the Christmas holidays, Blake School set on fire damaging the library, kitchen and cafeteria, several classrooms and the science block. Police were concerned that each fire was arson, but no one was ever caught.

1982

January Contractors moved into Hednesford on **Monday, January 25th** to start up to three months work on the town's sewerage system in Market Street which was to be closed except for deliveries. New pipes would be relayed along Market Street and some of Station Road because existing pipes were up to 60 years old and in danger of collapsing. The affected areas would be from Anglesey Street to Rugeley Road and between Green Heath Road and McGhie Street.

While that was being done work would begin on the Beehive Corner to make it safer. The road would be widened and a mini island at the bottom of Green Heath Road would be installed. A zebra crossing had been placed there some time ago, but it had not altered the congestion or made things safer for pedestrians.

In **April** the work was still nowhere near completion. It was then announced that it would take six months until **July 23rd** rather than the three because of trouble with the water mains which had to be diverted before

114. Beehive Corner c.1980.

new sewers could be laid. Hednesford traders began to lose patience and decided to protest by launching a pavement protest which included setting up shop outside. Passersby were offered a glass of wine while they browsed. In **August** the deadline was moved to late summer. Because of the loss of trade businessmen sought compensation from the Council, but they passed the buck on to Severn Trent Water Authority as it was their water mains that had caused all the problems. Needless to say compensation was not forthcoming!

To add to the Council's problems Hednesford traders said they would block any long term plans to make Market Street traffic free. Mr. Bates, President of the Hednesford and District Chamber of Trade and Commerce, said, "There is no way we want pedestrianisation."

★Your author firmly lays the demise of Hednesford shopping on this period of upheaval. As a regular shopper I noticed about ten shops which closed during those chaotic months and which never fully reopened. They have had trouble ever since with constant changes in ownership.

September The ageing St. Saviour's Church Hall in High Mount Street had to be demolished. The original hall was erected in 1920 when Charles Stacey, photographer in McGhie Street, transported sections, bought from the army camp for just £5, on a hand cart. The new hut would have heating, electrics and a fitted kitchen.

Historical note – St. Saviour's Church was opened in 1888 and in 1889 Thomas Wrench, shopkeeper, Peter Sharpe, cashier, and Robert Barton, builder, signed an indemnity agreement with Lichfield Diocese to keep the streets and pavements around the church in good order. In November/December 1901 services were held at West Hill Board School while the chancel was added. In 1903 the new organ was added and in 1922 the church was closed for redecoration and carpeting. The same took place in 1947/48. Finally around 1958 the vestry and organ loft were added.

November Rawnsley Foundry employed 24 men making a range of castings from pulleys to door knobs. The castings were made from sand moulds which were filled with molten iron. The manager, Lester Titley, said, "The system is antiquated but still has the best and cheapest way to make them." The factory was based on part of the old brickworks site which up until 1947 had been tied to Cannock Wood Colliery to make bricks for the pit and general use. When it closed down a group of foundry workers moved in, but a slump in the market in the 1950's saw it taken over by Tipper Industries Limited, a Willenhall firm. In 1970 that became part of Ductile Steels, also of Willenhall, but by August 1982 they had been taken over by the Glynwedd Group. The foundry's strength was its flexibility, making either a large amount of components or just a very small number; "as few as five," said Alan Taylor, the foreman.

Historical note – Hednesford Brickworks had a very long history. As early as the 1830's it was owned by the Foulke family and then in the 1840's by Thomas Cotton. You can follow the remainder of its nineteenth century history in the Census Reports. In 1920 Daniel Begley

115. Hednesford Brickworks.

116. Hednesford Brickworks.

was the general manager and by 1925 it was owned by Cannock Chase Colliery Company with S.F. Sopwith as general manager. In 1934 another continuous kiln was built and later two semi-continuous kilns were added. In 1938 six down draught kilns were added together with specialised machinery for various types of bricks. However, in 1939 with the War it closed and was used to store raw rubber. In 1947, like the mines, it was nationalised and after that made only bricks known as "commons". By the 1950's it was making over 16 million bricks per year and in 1953 a twenty chamber continuous kiln was set up, while in 1956 new underfed stokers were installed helping to make better quality bricks. The last manager was Mr. B. Roper before the works closed down some years ago.

December Tyler Mall Superstore opened in Wimblebury. Based on the American idea it saw different shops under one roof. However, by March, 1983 the mall had to call in the receiver for a second time. Thirteen businesses were still operating there and were thinking of setting up a co-operative to keep it open. It later became Chase Hyperdrome.

December The Council wanted to turn the West Cannock 5's Pit site into a light industrial place as had happened with the Cannock Wood Pit site. They would meet in the January to consider the proposition. The mine had closed on December 17th. It was the last of the mines in the Hednesford area.

1983

February Rawnsley families on the newly built Westgate and Middleway Estates complained of the ground beginning to sink due to the houses having been built on "swamp". Drains and paving slabs were sinking and in one case in Westgate a house was earmarked for demolition. Former councillor, Charles Taylor, said, "Before the homes were built water used to run over the site and the area is still very damp." Residents also complained of a nasty smell which might have been swamp gas. In **April** it was announced that families would be moved out to Chadsmoor while, if possible, houses would be taken apart and moved. However, it was found that numbers 9/10 Kempton Close and 1, 2 and 3 Middleway were not worth saving in their present position.

117. New Rawnsley houses 1960's.

By **February 1984** numbers 9/10 Kempton Close had been relocated to a site just off Princess Street, Chadsmoor.

By **1988** over a hundred properties needed work doing on them. With around £10,000 needed to be spent on each house the Council applied to the government for a loan which was granted. The main trouble with the houses was that they had been built largely from wood.

June Mr. Morris, the 69 year old owner of the Raceway, announced that he was going to shut it over a dispute with the Council. He objected to paying rates and rent in the winter months when there was no racing. In July the Council discussed possible new rates and also what could be done with the site in the winter months – boot sales or auctions were possibilities.

1984

March There was a call for a comprehensive plan for the future of Hednesford town centre, like those of Bridgtown and Cannock, but the Council said it could not be done with present work commitments. Again there were mumblings of Hednesford being sacrificed for the good of Cannock!

However, in **April** it was announced that Hednesford was to get a £200,000 "shot in the arm" with a major pedestrianised shopping precinct which aimed to inject new life into the Church Hill side of the town. To make room one of the remaining buildings from the "shanty town" was to be demolished (No. 9 Market Street). There would be a complex of shops and offices reached via an archway and added to that a new car maintenance centre would be built on the former factory site in Uxbridge Street. The project was proposed by Mr. J. Donnelly who had already persuaded some shop owners to take units.

★Those proposals went ahead with the units being built at the rear and side of the Uxbridge Arms. They lasted a very short time with the office spaces never being taken up. Mr. Donnelly left the area not long after! The offices had a chequered history, but at least one unit is in operation today as the Boogaloo Cafe. However, the car site was a success and still operates today.

April A scheme earmarked since the 1970's for Hawkes Green, just on Hednesford's boundary, was given the go-ahead. By 1991 some 2,500 houses, shops and a public house were to be built. There would also be a petrol station and land for a new school if it was needed. The site was bounded by Lichfield Road in the south, Gorsemoor Road in the east, Hednesford Canal Basin in the west and Hill Street in the north. By **July** they were already "making good" the old canal basin site which, when completed in 1985, would provide over thirty two acres for industry as well as playing fields.

May British Rail backed a move for the revival of train services from Hednesford having received a petition of over 5,500 signatures. It could be as early as summer 1985. However, the County Council could not afford the cost of renovating the line.

August 24th Councillor John O'Leary performed the opening ceremony of the new scenic park on the former tip in Stafford Lane. The sixteen acre site had been transformed into walkways with trees and a landscaped pool, at a cost of £170,000.

1985

January It was announced that a rail service could be operating by the spring. Around £197,000 had been put aside by the County Council for the reopening and building of new stations, but that might not be sufficient. In November, 1986 British Rail's latest offer was to run an hourly service which would involve less money from the County Council. Local action groups petitioned them to accept the offer.

March The Council had ideas for the Valley Pit site which would include a village green, a football pitch and all weather pitches. Local community groups would also be allowed to use the existing buildings for various activities. A car park for 90 vehicles was also envisaged. Industrial usage was ruled out.

In the January the National Coal Board had informed the Council that they were willing to sell off the Valley Pit site to be used for recreational purposes. (They had already sold the Grove site in Norton Canes for leisure activities.)

Historical note – The Valley Pit had become a training pit for new recruits in 1947. In 1971 the Mines Rescue Station closed in Victoria Street and moved to the old baths site at the Valley Pit. In 1978 the training centre closed followed by the rescue station in 1984.

February The Aquarius had undergone a refurbishment and as Hednesford had no Council owned premises in the town a neighbourhood office was set up there where people could pay their rates or rents.

July 19th To attract more shoppers into the town Hednesford traders arranged a Folk Festival day. There would be folk dancing, puppets and hobby horse dancing along with a craft fair. Music would happen throughout the two day event. In the same month, for the more adventurous there would be a BMX road race around Market Street, Eskrett Street and Anglesey Street and a "vintage car" competition as well as a motorcycle display in a purposely set up museum.

1986

November A report on the state of Hednesford said that a great deal of redevelopment had taken place either to replace old buildings or totally refurbish them. A policy of not duplicating types of outlet had led to a wide variety of shops. Unfortunately the same could not be said for Station Road where shop owners complained of "crumbling, potholed pavements". They were furious at the state of the railway bridge leading into the town where pavements were too narrow, forcing people into the road. As one shopkeeper said, "You regularly see mums with pushchairs having to step into the road." The council said that work was to start on resurfacing the pavements, but

118. Station Road 2010.

119. Sunday demonstration in Station Road.

widening them would cost too much as it might mean building a new separate footbridge. It was unlikely that finances would be available.

November British Rail's latest offer was to run an hourly service which would involve less money from the County Council. Local actions groups hoped that the County would not back out.

1987

April The Cannock Chase Enterprise Scheme on the old No. 5's Pit site had already been created with more than 100 jobs provided with 47 industrial units. The disused buildings had been refurbished to hold small businesses and the road access to the site was being improved. The centre had been in operation since October, 1986. The other major aspect of the scheme would be a one million pound contract to reclaim and restore the nearby 250 acres of the former colliery site from an "eyesore" to green open space.

By **May, 1989** the area had finally been reclaimed with the addition of pleasant walks and pools. The soil heaps of the old colliery had been grassed over and planted with trees.

April Residents of Brindley Heath complained of a "second class service". The Council replied by saying that over five million had been spent on the village since it came under the District Council with over £300,000 spent on play areas. A bus service had been introduced (the Green Bus), but had been stopped due to lack of support. In **May, 1988** the Council agreed to renovate the bungalows putting in a modern heating system, new windows and doors and roof repairs. They had acted because people were unwilling to move into them because of the "unattractive appearance" of the homes.

July Bomb alert! Whilst bulldozing the area for an extension to the Automatic Transmissions factory an unexploded bomb was unearthed – a mortar shell with half a pound of explosives. The Army Disposal Unit was called in and it was detonated on site. Whilst there they discovered a second device, an anti tank shell, on Friday 11th and it was removed for detonation. From July 13th/20th the site was closed off again for further searches, but no other devices were found. Richard Hathaway, Promotions Manager at ATP, said, "It certainly disrupted our business and caused a bit of excitement among the staff."

120. *Automatic Transmissions factory.*

Speculation as to how the devices got on the site led to the possibility of them being left there when the Drill Hall had been the training centre for the Territorial Army.

November The Department of Transport had allocated £210,000 to build new stations at Hednesford, Cannock and Landywood, but that fund had not been used by the County Council. Actions groups said that it should be used quickly or the money might be lost. The County's response was that government cutbacks had meant the delay as the County Council could not afford to match the government offer as was expected. County Councillor Dix said, "There is no chance of starting before the end of next April because we have got no resources."

December The opening ceremony of St. Peter's new church took place led by Bishop Mayfield of Wolverhampton. Old St. Peter's had been demolished in 1986 because of the effects of subsidence over the years.

121. *Construction of the new St. Peter's Church.*

1988

February The residents of Woodlands Close and Bradbury Lane complained to the Council over the state of their homes. Built in 1947/48 they still had the original windows and doors. As there was no money left in the budget for that year the Council refused to do anything.

March British Rail's scheme for an hourly train service was finally given the go-ahead after a seven year campaign. Staffordshire County Council had finally agreed after British Rail had reduced operating and capital costs for the service and four new stations.

November Major roadworks were announced for the Old Hednesford Road as part of the eastern bypass. It was also hoped to

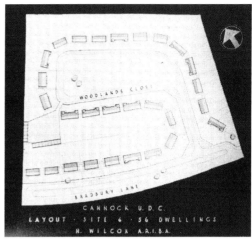

122. Plan of Woodland Close.

prevent future flooding, especially under the railway bridge. The work would take two weeks.

1989

January Moors Gorse Pumping Station was to be upgraded and after that the plant could supply water to the area should the electricity fail as had happened in October, 1987.

123. Moor's Green Pumping Station.

February Plans were put forward for a new traffic island outside St. Joseph's School at Hill Top. Part of the wasteland outside the school had been earmarked for an island. The main problem was parking for the parents. Father Brown suggested that land opposite the school on the corner of Stafford Lane might be used as a car park. As we know that is exactly what happened.

February A fire gutted the former Blake Lower School, High Town which had been up for sale. It took forty firemen over seven hours to bring it under control. Their problem had been that all the windows and doors were boarded up and access was very difficult. Almost the whole of the building had been gutted. At the end three firemen had been injured. It was thought that the fire had been started deliberately by young arsonists who were seen near the building. Police investigated but never found the culprits.

June The Council opened the Valley Heritage Centre on the site of the old Valley Pit. The old pony stores and offices became the museum itself while various other buildings were used for commercial activities. The baths eventually became a restaurant which burnt down in 2002. The burnt out building was demolished in May, 2003 and used for housing. The cycle sheds became a craft centre with a blacksmith, Valley Forge, and a Stained Glass Studio. In time the whole site would become the Museum of Cannock Chase which in 2013 was taken over by Wigan Leisure.

June St. Michael's Church, Rawnsley celebrated its centenary.

Historical note – St. Michael's Church had started life as St. John's Iron Church and was licensed to worship on December 23rd, 1889. A fund was then started to provide a bell and harmonium. The old tin mission soon became too small and so the vicar of St. Peter's, Reverend John Reay, arranged for the purchase of an army hut from the Camps. Cannock and Rugeley Colliery Company donated the land, thousands of bricks and helped in its construction. April, 1922 the new gas lit church was dedicated and in 1947 a new altar was installed, dedicated to the eight local men who lost their lives in the War. By 1970 £2,200 had been raised to help build a new church and church hall, but it was to be another twelve years before those plans came to fruition. The crucifix attached to the front wall of the new church came from St. Paul's Church, Wimblebury. The new church was dedicated on March 27th, 1982.

The Nineties
(1990 - 1999)

1990

February Residents along Rugeley Road near to the town complained about the lorry park on the corner of Victoria Street and Rugeley Road saying that it was too near the town centre and spoilt the view of the park and the Hills. They said it would be better used as a car park.

March Property developer, Mr. Ken Lees of Cannock based KGL, wanted to demolish the Cross Keys Inn as part of a £3.5 million plan for the area. He said that he intended to rebuild, making private flats and build it as a replica of the old inn. The Keys Football Ground at the rear would be made into a housing estate and the club moved to a new site. Mr. Lees said, "The empty building had been blighted by vandals, suffered from mining subsidence and was unsafe." Councillor Nigel Sidebottom said of the plans, "It would be merely a replica. It is a futile gesture." In **April** the Council deferred the decision until further structural survey had been done. In the meantime they ordered work to be carried out to prevent further deterioration. They had received a petition of 450 signatures and 515 letters protesting against the demolition. Several agencies, like English Heritage, were against the plans, but at the time were not sure of success.

124. Cross Keys Inn c.1910.

In the 1950's repairs had been carried out on the floors of the inn and had revealed an old cock fighting pit scattered with feathers. In March, 1973 it had been listed as being of special architectural interest and of historical interest and given a Grade II status.

Fortunately as we know the building stayed. The football club did move to its new site on Keys Park Road and the new housing estate, Keys Close, was built.

March Yet another historically important building seemed to be under threat when the Anglesey Hotel lost its ability to operate as an inn. The tenants were informed by Health and Safety officials that they had to have a separate kitchen to prepare meals for customers in addition to the family one. Bass, Mitchells and Butlers had recently spent money redecorating the exterior and would not spend any more. They said it was the tenant's responsibility to refurbish the interior. It would mean the eventual closure of the inn and the building being taken over by Pritchard Holdings. Today its new owners are Wetherspoons who finished their refurbishment with added kitchen and storage space at the side in 2015.

125. Views in Hednesford c.1910.

April Hednesford Raceway was completely gutted by fire over the weekend of 14/15th. The fire wiped out the twenty five year old Bromford Bridge grandstand and the adjacent restaurant and bar. With it went the race control office, the power and the public address system. Despite that the Easter Meeting still continued.

September Residents of Pye Green Road gathered a 300 strong petition to stop local farmland being used as a refuse dump. They feared that the five acre site might be used for factory units. Mr. Eric Holford, owner, said that only bricks and subsoil were being deposited and after one year's use he would turn the area into recreational use.

October 13th On that Friday a crater appeared in the road at Church Hill and ruined the bungalow nearby, fracturing water mains. The owners said their life had been blighted by subsidence and wanted British Coal to take responsibility. They could not sell their home because of the constant fear. British Coal filled the hole with concrete and repaired the bungalow.

The old Church Hill Working Men's Club which had stood on the corner of Church Hill and New Street for almost a hundred years was demolished along with the two terraced houses that were next door. They were next to the bungalow. A car park for the newly built club was created at the front of the building.

1991

January Dowty Electronics along Rugeley Road which made magnetic sensors and systems for the defence industry announced that they were to lose a quarter of their workforce due to increase in costs. They employed 74 people.

January With the closure of Littleton Colliery slurry from the works was transported to the old brickworks site in Hednesford. Residents in Stafford Lane complained that, instead of working at weekends, they were moving it by lorry during the week causing noise and disturbance all day.

January The Council were in favour of plans to convert the Grade 11 listed Prospect House into a new public house and four small apartments. The building was in need of repair and renovation. The new building with car park would be hidden from the estate being constructed in Keys Place. For more of the history of that old house see your author's book *Hednesford's Horse Racing History.*

126. Prospect House c.1950.

February Plans to extend the rail link to Rugeley and Stafford had been discussed, but with the "lack of investment" by British Rail the government might stop them. In **May** it was announced that a new service straight through to Birmingham would start in the July. It would mean passengers would no longer have to change at Walsall. The Council was also to decide on the extension to Rugeley.

February On February 19th the first sod was cut on Hednesford Hills for the new reservoir. The contractors, Shepherd's Hill, said that the four million gallon reservoir was essential to guarantee water for Hednesford, Cannock and Rugeley. It would also ensure that a "sensible and sympathetic" landscaping would be created to protect the look of the Hills. Hednesford Hills Preservation Society, whose chairman was Mr. Waltho, was not happy saying, "The valley will no longer be a valley as the construction rises, but the reservoir is now a fact of life."

*In fact if you walk up the valley from the Museum of Cannock Chase towards the old reservoir at the top you will hardly notice that the new reservoir is there.

April Mr. Norman Round, owner of the White House on Marquis Drive, had been given permission to convert the restaurant into a 16 bedroom hotel. However, his new plans were to demolish the restaurant and build a 42 bedroom hotel. The Council refused permission and so he appealed to the government agency.

May Chetwynd Mining and Piling Company had purchased the Cross Keys Inn from KLG in 1990 and had put forward plans to restore the public house and convert the old stables and barn site into a restaurant and bedrooms to open alongside the inn. Those had been accepted and work was in full progress. They hoped to open in August. Mr. Peake said, "After removing the dangerous ceiling in the former concert room the roof contained very old oak trusses and purlins. Infilling with brickwork and plaster on one of the beams proved "conclusively" that the pub dated from Tudor times."

For further history of the Cross Keys Inn see your author's book *"A History of Hednesford and Surrounding Villages"*.

127. Cross Keys repairs.

November The new plans announced for Hednesford town centre would involve a one-way system from Anglesey Street to Rugeley Road with extra parking outside shops, raised crossing points for pedestrians and a variety of environmental improvements, including trees, benches and a large water feature near the Anglesey Hotel. Road improvements on Rugeley Road and its junction with Victoria Street had already been approved. In July, 1992 the plans were given the go-ahead and a possible 20 mph speed limit was discussed.

1992

January Allied Bakeries who owned Stantons announced that 74 jobs could go owing to new EC regulations. Their refrigeration plant was not viable and it meant that pasties and sausage rolls could no longer be made there.

February ATP Industries were fined for an oil spillage into Ridings Brook which fed into Mill Green Pool. It had happened when oil was being transferred from one tank to another. ATP paid for the clean-up which cost £879 and made a donation to the RSPCA. To stop it happening again they built a retaining wall round the tanks.

April Plans were submitted to the Council to convert the deserted offices at the rear of the Uxbridge Arms, Consort Court, which had remained virtually empty since their construction in 1984, into a twenty room motel. The Council approved the plans. Unfortunately those rooms were barely used, except by the DSS, and still remain virtually unoccupied today.

July Proposals seemed afoot to move the War Memorial into the centre of Hednesford opposite the Anglesey Hotel. It would be part of the £300,000 development announced earlier. The plans were met with strong opposition, including the Royal British Legion. Salvation Army Band member Mr. Maurice Baskeyfield said, "The present site speaks volumes for the past. I think our forefathers thought very carefully before selecting the site. It is unique because most memorials are in town centres with all the bustling traffic of the day."

128. War Memorial c.1950.

In August the Council announced that it would not be moved and laid the blame on the local press who had seen fit to interview older residents before checking on the facts.

August Residents living on the fringes of Hednesford Hills complained about the spraying of the bracken being carried out by the Forestry Commission, fearing for their health and that of wildlife. They were assured that it was "not harmful to humans or animals" and the Forestry Commission was supported by the Hednesford Hills Preservation Society who realised the Hills were being destroyed by the bracken. The same spraying would happen in Sherbrook Valley later.

September Just after 5 a.m. on Monday September 14th a blaze damaged part of the White House on the Chase. Four fire crews finally brought it under control, but not before the offices and kitchen were destroyed. The restaurant was saved, but the damaged area had to be demolished. The fire was blamed on a possible electrical fault underneath the wooden staircase of the two storey building.

September Fears over further subsidence on Church Hill prompted moves to restrict heavy goods vehicles from using the hill. Local bus companies were asked not to use the route and delivery companies were to be written to asking them to find other routes. In **January, 1994** the Council decided that heavy goods vehicles would not be banned.

129. Stanton's Bakery.

September Stantons Bakery was to close altogether with the loss of 275 jobs on October 24th. The announcement came by fax from Allied Bakeries. It read:- "The change in shopping patterns and the move to in-store baking had resulted in a lower proportion of our sales being dependant on our retail plant bakery. We regret this will cause redundancies at a difficult time."

1993

March Work began on the strengthening of Hednesford Railway Bridge brought about by the increase of traffic over the old wrought iron and timber bridge. Work had also begun on the improvements to Market Street. It had been decided to replace the water feature outside the Anglesey Hotel with a tower clock.

April There was a rededication service held at the Soldiers Institute in Anglesey Street of the plaque for those territorial soldiers who fought in the Boer War. A church parade at 11.00 a.m. was followed by the rededication. The plaque had originally been in the Drill Hall.

130. Reconstruction of Hednesford Bridge.

June It was announced that the rail link to Rugeley could open as soon as May 1994 if Cannock Council could find the money. Over 100,000 passengers had used the service from

Hednesford in the 1992/93 period which boded well for the extension. However, in September British Rail wanted to stop two of the midday services due to the increase of coal wagons. In December they said the link to Rugeley would be "frozen". No decision would be made by British Rail because in April, 1994 the government would bring in privatisation and the link to Rugeley was causing engineering problems due to the station being on a slope.

July Hednesford Traders were considering suing the Council over the loss of business due to the redevelopment of Market Street. That followed a heated meeting with the Council where their worries were ignored. There would be no rate relief, despite a drop in trade. At least five small businesses had gone under since its start in March.

July Councillor John Burnett complained about the state of ATP's factory site in Victoria Street. He claimed they were in breach of the storage conditions and car parking space agreement they had made with the Council. He said they had made a "pathetic attempt at landscaping the site" and "stillages which were there had not been moved for three years". The bosses at ATP said they had recently won a contract for the remanufacture of gearboxes with Chrysler International of America and their storage efforts had been thrown out of gear. However, they planned a belt of conifers to screen the site from the road. Permission to delay organising the site was granted provided the conifers were in by November 30th and the open storage problem solved within a year.

September Led by Mrs. Margaret Riddell the residents of Hazel Slade petitioned the authorities to register land off Cannock Wood Street as a village green. Downs Homes had applied to the Council to build 14 houses on the land. British Coal who owned the land, known locally as The Rec, said it had been a farm within the last twenty years which made it ineligible to be a village green. Residents claimed it had not been ploughed since the 1920's. In March, 1994 the authorities found in favour of the villagers.

November Protests, which would last many years, began over the construction of a road through Pye Green Valley to serve the possible new housing on the site. ★See my earlier comments.

1994

January Developers Persimmon Ltd. submitted plans to build up to forty houses on the old Stanton's Bakery site. Despite the local residents of Western Road being against them permission was eventually granted in August, 1996 by the Council for fifty four houses.

March It was announced that Hednesford Football Club was hoping to move to its new ground on part of the site of the old brickworks at the rear of houses in Hill Street. Local residents, backed by Heath Hayes Parish Council, objected but permission was granted. The owners had been given instructions to landscape the area and screen the ground from the houses. In January, 1995, having already begun its construction, the Football Club wanted permission to increase the height of the stand from 7 meters to 11 and open from 9 a.m. until 11.30 p.m. on match days and again the Council agreed. In the February gas leakages from the old site (probably methane) forced the Club to build the 620 seater stand on one meters high stilts. By April, 1995 it had been decided to name the ground Keys Park to start the new 1995/96 season. The final game at the Cross Keys Ground would be played on May 9/10th. Sir Stanley Matthews opened the Keys Park on November, 6th, 1995.

October Plans to build a warehouse and loading bay at A.T.P. in Victoria Street, which had been approved in July 1991, were given the go-ahead. (Construction had already started.)

131. A.T.P. factory warehouse and loading bay.

October Hednesford Hills was declared a nature reserve to protect rare heathland. In July 1991 Staffordshire Heathland Partnership had been set up by English Nature and official registration was given to the Hills.

1995

February Moves by Royal Mail to take Hednesford from the postal address were met with local opposition. Councillor Ball said, "Hednesford has a separate identity and I would ask all residents to use it or lose it." It was also argued that same street names in the area would cause confusion if just "Cannock" were used. By September, 1996 it seemed likely that some names would disappear as the Royal Mail was moving to a new computer system and it only needed post codes to operate.

February Owners of the quarry on Rugeley Road applied for permission to increase lorry activity from 50 to 100 per day. They needed the increase as they had a five year plan to stabilise the quarry slopes following several accidents at the site. Brindley Heath Parish Council objected, but it was granted.

March Plans were put forward to build 240 houses in Pye Green Valley at the top of Green Heath Road and 40 more at the bottom. Councillor Hill argued that "once completed the site will regenerate the local economy in Hednesford, Chadsmoor and Pye Green". A petition of over 2,000 raised objections to the scheme.

April West Hill School unveiled its six new classrooms in a two storey building. Way back in 1919 the girls school had been destroyed by fire and "temporary" classrooms had been built from old military huts off the Chase until the new school could be built.

*Summer madness? It was the year for strange sightings! First it was reports of a wild cat roaming the Chase and then came the

132. West Hill School's new block.

U.F.O's! Unfortunately no pictures were ever captured of the panther/leopard, but once the band wagon began to roll.....

September The Council announced that the spoil tip opposite Hednesford Town Football Club was to be redeveloped to create an industrial park. British Coal Properties, which would cease to exist in 1996, owned the site, but part of their agreement when releasing it was to restore the site.

October Residents of Wimblebury Road complained about the Marquis Park Estate which had been constructed by Veletrose Limited in 1989. It was still incomplete with no true roads, footpaths or street lighting. The company said they would complete when all house sales had happened. (The housing slump was to blame.) In the same month the Council agreed to develop the Capital nightspot site in Wimblebury to include public open spaces, ponds and walkways. It would act as a buffer zone to stop any further development from the Anglesey Business Park on Littleworth Road.

1996

February Some residents of Hednesford, especially along Green Heath Road, denied wanting a Hednesford Parish Council just to stop the road being built in Pye Green Valley. They had contacted Staffordshire Parish Councils Association in December 1995 about the idea. Mrs. Ann Turville, a leading light, said, "We have no interest in local politics." Ironic then that when we finally did have a parish council both she and her husband stood for election.

February Plans were submitted for Wimblebury to get 276 new houses on the old brickworks site. However, the Council were not in favour due to the lack of school places in the area. Instead in the November they gave permission for an £8.8 million scheme to transform the old site into a business park.

February Between Christmas and February the Valley Heritage Centre was vandalised no less than seven times, the last one causing some £5,000 worth of damage when a St. John's Ambulance unit was burned out.

February A £50,000 scheme was announced to improve Hednesford between Hednesford Station and the Market Car Park. It included landscaping, environmental improvement to the market place and ground floor improvement to Market Street buildings. The visible signs nowadays are the steps leading down into the car park behind the Co-op and flower beds either side.

March The old Cross Keys Football Ground and area around was to be turned into a housing estate with 44 new homes. The developers made a promise to make a contribution to Hednesford Park and upgrade Prospect House, a grade two listed building.

August It was announced that the rail link to Rugeley would finally open in March, 1997 after a 33 year wait. There would be a new platform at Hednesford and it would be an hourly service. It finally opened in June, 1997. On Friday May 30th an inaugural train ran from Rugeley to Hednesford and the service began on Monday June 2nd.

September Hednesford Market looked as if it were dying on its feet as there were only four stallholders left. Eight stalls had closed during the preceding three months and the site was in a poor condition. Like other places in the area it had been hit by vandalism.

October Residents of Rowley Close complained that their estate was "forgotten" as many street lights were not working, footpaths were all churned up, children had nowhere to play and vandals had ruined the area.

December On Friday evening, December 20th, at about 8.45 p.m. a fire broke out at

Hednesford Park Sports Pavilion. It took twenty firemen to control the blaze which began in the attic and it was thought to be another case of arson. It left the Council with an estimated bill of £200,000.

133. Hednesford Park Pavilion c.1960.

1997

February Plans were put forward by Mr. Eric Holford to build a stable and tack room next to Hazel Slade School on the Rugeley Road. Some locals objected because they thought the children might be injured by the horses. However, in May permission was granted, provided he placed a bank next to the school fencing to act as a buffer.

March Hednesford lost its case to have security cameras for Market Street. The funding from the Home Office was not forthcoming, but traders could reapply in the June. Feeling let down by Cannock Council some traders organised a survey asking Hednesford residents if they felt let down by the Council. Of the more than 300 who responded over 90% were unhappy with the Council's commitment to Hednesford. In July it was announced that the new government had shelved plans for further CCTV funding. Chris Collins, Chairman of Hednesford Traders, said, "While we wait vandalism and crime continues. Hardly a day goes by without a window being smashed or property damaged."

On Saturday June 14th between 8.80 p.m. and 9.00 p.m. the arsonists struck again when they set fire to a stall in the market. ★Thought to be the work of adolescents, damage had been done round the area for some time.

May Over one hundred people objected to a waste station and recycling centre being situated at the old Bestmore site along the Rugeley Road. The Council were all for it as it would only be used for paper, wood and metal.

May Hednesford's cash bonanza! It was announced that £300,000 was to be spent on upgrading Hednesford Park; an estimated £7 million investment plan to reclaim the old brickworks site; and improvements to the Heritage Centre in Valley Road. The Council would also remove the outdoor market as so few people used it.

August Arsonists struck for the third time at Hednesford Park pavilion just days before the

£90,000 repair scheme was to begin. The blaze was reported just after 9.00 p.m. on Saturday 23rd and swept through the building. There had been a suspicious fire only three weeks previously.

October Plans for the stables on Rugeley Road, Hazel Slade were given the go-ahead. As the site was bounded by Hazel Slade Nature Reserve no commercial business could take place which restricted riding lessons, trapping or livery. Any waste was to be stored and the disposed of.

1998

January Finally the go-ahead was given for CCTV in Hednesford by the Council and plans would go to the County Council in March. However, in July the government once again rejected the plans despite a petition of over 800 names.

January Plans were submitted to build a further 19 stables at Stafford Brook Farm at the end of Cotswold Road. The owners said the site would be screened and cars could exit the site using Brindley Heath Road. The 135 acre site already had 50 stables and so the application was rejected as it "would stick out like a sore thumb" in an area of outstanding natural beauty. In August Mr. Goodman, a government inspector, said the Council had been "unreasonable" and the plans to build further stables and two fishing lakes were "not contrary to plans for protecting the green belt".

June During their rebuilding of the park pavilion builders, Three Pines of Wolverhampton, had fencing ripped up and a door to one mobile unit knocked down.

July A nine hole extension to Beaudesert Golf Course was passed. It would be close to Hednesford Quarry.

August Plans to move what remained of the historic racing stables at Hazel Slade to further down the valley opposite Rawnsley Road were deferred due to the presence of voles in Bentley Brook. The application was to build 15 stables, a store room, tack room and a car park. Nature experts would check the site and report back. In September it said the plans could go ahead if

134. Hazel Slade racing stables.

the site was moved ten metres back from the river bank to protect the voles. The only concern then was the limited access to the water for the horses. In October the plans were agreed. The developers also agreed to contribute to pedestrian/cycle track to run alongside the disused railway track next to the stables.

*For the complete history of the Hazel Slade Stables see *Hednesford's Horse Racing History.*

September Councillor Les Bullock claimed that Wimblebury was "dying from the heart" owing to the amount of new housing in the area while "virtually nothing had been put into the village (by way of amenities) except to make it a vast dormitory for the area". That followed an application to build 9 more homes at Watermead as part of a further 275 house development. He claimed "people just used the village to sleep".

October A petition to see whether Hednesford wanted a Parish Council was started and soon got over 4,000 names in support. Surprisingly Hednesford was the only place in the area, apart from Cannock, not to have one. In August, 1999 it was announced that it would get its Parish Council starting in 2000.

December Proposed parish boundary changes, which were necessary because of large scale building on the eastern side of Hednesford, would place Hednesford Football Ground in Heath Hayes. A row would rumble on for nearly a year until it was finally decided to leave it where it had always been.

1999

April Plans for the stables opposite Rawnsley Road were finally given to go-ahead. They would include 15 stables and a four bedroomed house for staff and visitors. The only stipulation put on the building was that it must remain as stables if it went up for sale in the future.

June Despite protests from residents of Sharon Way about the size of the building Jewson opened their distribution warehouse on the old brickworks site. It would employ over 100 people. To appease the local residents Jewson paid some £2,500 to retune televisions in the area.

July Another perennial problem – fires on Hednesford Hills! Starting at 11 a.m. on Saturday 17th the fire brigade were called out fourteen times in twenty four hours. Once again blame was attributed to youngsters.

September The park pavilion was finally opened with four changing rooms and a meeting room.

November Tesco announced that they were to build a 10 million pound supermarket in Hednesford.

A Twenty First Century Picturebook

I thought I might end the book with a quick look in pictures at some of the developments in Hednesford since 2000. You, like me, may be surprised just how long ago some of these events happened. It is surprising just how quickly our exact memories fade.

2005 Hednesford Valley Clinic opened. Most of the doctors on the west side of Hednesford decided to combine clinics in one building. *Strictly speaking the valley never had that name, but it does stand in a valley next to the railway and so is apt.

2005 The demolition of Pool Cottage in Victoria Street opposite Hednesford Park. Now the site of the new bingo hall and various shops it was originally built in 1913 and stood on Pool View.

2006 The first phase of the Miners' Memorial was dedicated by Bishop Michael Bourke of Wolverhampton on July 29th. The brainchild of CHAPS whose president was Tony Wright M.P. and Jack Sunley it depicts the names of colliery workers and the mine where they worked most of their lives in bricks paid for by their families. Later additions happened in 2012 (below) and 2014 (top of following page) and were placed around the town clock. In its central position in Hednesford it has created a great deal of interest, probably more than any other memorial in the area.

2006 "Lowlands" at the rear of the old post office in Market Street and what was once Howard Ball's men's clothing shop was demolished and a block of flats built in 2008. ★For many years it had been the home and surgery of Doctor Stooke who had been there before World War Two. Before that it had been lived in by Doctor S. Smith.

2007 School Court Residential Home was built in Station Road on the site of the old Valley Infants School which had stood there since 1903.

2008 The demolition of Blagg's shop and construction of Church Hill Mews caused much local opposition when the building contractors originally wanted to name it Rugeley Buildings. ★The hardware store had stood there for over a century, run by members of the same family. For more information on the store see *A History of Hednesford and Surrounding Villages.*

2008 Pritchard Holdings began work on converting the old Moore's and Joseph Lucas Factory in Market Street into the Light Works. The first floor would be converted into flats while below on the ground floor it would be retail outlets. A small museum/eatery was envisaged at the far end though that never came to fruition as Pritchard Holdings eventually had to sell the building to private landlords.

2010 Alterations to the site of Pool House in Victoria Street (not to be confused with Pool Cottage). It had originally been the home of the Owen family who ran the Hednesford Hills Mineral Water Company, later known as Gem Pop Factory run by Thomas Cashin who had married into the family. The business had been started just after 1900 by the Owen brothers and T. Owen ran it until after the Second World War. The house was finally demolished to make way for the new Victoria Street development.

2010 Work began on constructing a roundabout at High Town to ease the flow of traffic at the junction of Cannock Road, Stafford Lane and Belt Road. Strangely planners were somewhat amazed when they uncovered a bridge at the site. ★Most elderly residents could have told them that it was built in the 1870's to allow trucks to take coal from West Cannock No. 1 and 3 Pits to the railway yard at Hednesford. Another clue to its presence may have been the Bridge Inn at High Town.

2011/12 The redevelopment of Victoria Street, Rugeley Road and parts of Market Street began with the demolition of the ATP Factory, Drill Hall, Aquarius, bus station and various shops and houses along those stretches to be used. The first buildings to be complete were those now occupied by the new bingo hall and various shop outlets in Market Street whilst the Tesco's store finally opened in December, 2012. Aldi's store followed in early 2013 as did the new Aquarius building.

2014 The railway bridge at the bottom of Bradbury Lane was demolished in January and a new one built by May to accommodate the electrification of the railway line to Rugeley. Also done at the same time was the bridge leading up to the Chase Enterprise site (Walkers' Rise). Further along the line at Moors Green the level crossing was replaced by a bridge going over the line for cyclists and walkers.

Appendix 1

OCCUPANTS OF MARKET STREET 1914 – 1938

★ Right hand side looking from Churchill.

	1914	1920	1929	1938
2.	T.J. Hill (draper)	T.J. Hill	J. Clarke (draper)	Bon Marche
4.	H. Hill (butcher)	H. Hill	H. Hill	F.E. Owen (butcher)
6.	H. Stubbs (dairyman)	H.Stubbs (cafe)	C. Harthill (tobacco)	S.A. Boycott (fancy goods)
8.	C. Bradbury (clothier)	M.Biningsley (fish/fruit)	?	?
10.	Miss Bradbury (dresses)	Becomes EMPTY SPACE		
12.		OPEN SPACE for ADVERTISING.		
14.	Mrs. Davies	Mrs. Davies	Peakes (furniture)	Peakes
16.	G. Tranter (pork butcher)	G. Tranter	G. Tranter	G. Tranter
18.	Bailey Bros. (tailors)	Bailey Bros.	?	?
20.	Mrs. Bishop (baker)	Mrs. Bishop	G.Hartnell	A.Tribali (sweets/choc.)
22.	A.J. Holland (fancy goods)	A.J. Holland	A.J. Holland	A.J. Holland
24.	W.S. Jones (cycles/music)	W.S.Jones	W.S.Jones	W.S. Jones
26.	G. Dando (fruit)	G. Dando	?	?
28.	J. Frisby (bootmaker)	J. Frisby	J. Frisby	J. Frisby
30.	J. Brindley (fried fish)	J. Brindley	J. Brindley	?
32.	J. Ratcliffe (butcher)	J. Ratcliffe	J. Ratcliffe	G. Merrett (butcher)
34.	G. Smith (draper)	G. Smith	G. Smith	?
36.	E. Webb (watchmaker)	E. Webb	E. Webb	T.Williams (sweets/tob.)
38.	Co-op Stores	Co-op Stores	E.Hardwick (grocer)	Prog. Club
40.	Progressive Club	Prog. Club	Prog. Club	E.J. Merritt (woolshop)
42.	E. Pope (fish/fruit)	M.A. Pope (fish/fruit)	W. Elliott	?
44.	A. Jones (cycles)	A. Jones/E.L. Merrett	E. Merrett (draper)	
46.	Maypole Dairy Co.	Maypole Co.	Maypole Co.	Maypole Co.

	1914	1920	1929	1938
48.	Hed.W.M.Club	Hed.Club	Club	Club
50.	F.Allen	A.D.Wimbush (confect.)		
52.	F.Allen (butcher)	F.Allen	?	Johnson (dry cleaners)
54.	F.Smith (draper/boots)	F.W. Smith	S.E. Smith	Craners (clothiers)
56.	W.Douglas (tailor/clothes)	Melias Ltd. (grocer)	Melias	Melias
58.	W.Douglas (tailor/clothes)	W.Douglas	?	Carters (draper)
60.	F.Briggs (bootmaker)	F.Briggs	?	Dewhursts (butcher)
62.	R.Waterworth (fruit)	H.Gee	A.A.Rose (hauliers)	R.Hewitt (gen. stores)
64.	H.Gee (leather)	H.Gee	H.Gee (fruit)	Taylors (fruit)
66.	A.Payne (baker/tobacco)	A.Payne	J.Iken (confect/tob)	J.Iken
68.	R.Whittle (chemist)	R.Whittle	R.Whittle	R.Whittle
68a.	S.Taylor (baker/confect.)	H.Levine (draper)		
70.	F.Cotterill (milliner)	M.Grosvenor (milliner)	M.Grosvenor	A.Shaw (milliner)
72.	Foster Bros. (clothiers)	Foster Bros.	Foster Bros.	Foster Bros.
74.	W.Webster (butcher)	W.Webster	W.Webster	F.Haycock (butcher)
76.	Hed.Advertiser Office	Hed.Advertiser	?	?
78.	S.Hall (ironmonger)	S.Hall	S.Hall (furniture etc.)	C.Hall
80.	B.Evans (printer/station)	B.Evans	B.Evans	F.H.Lowery (newsag.)
82.	C.Bailey (draper)+	C.W.Bailey	C.W.Bailey	C.W.Bailey
	Metropolitan Bank	Midland Bank	Midland Bank	Midland Bank
84/90	MARKET HALL ★H.Sleath leased the Market Hall from 1914 – 1930's.			
90.	Mrs Mellor (gen/beer)	Mrs. Mellor	?	Sleath Stores (fruit)
92.	A.Carroll (clothier)	A.Carroll	Bailey Bros.	Bailey Bros.
94.	W.R. Ives (wines/spirits)	W.R. Ives	Ives/Nock Ltd.	Ives/Nock Ltd.
96.	C.Ellisson (chemist)	C.Ellisson	R.L.Williams (chem.)	R.L.Williams
98.	J.Bagnell (cafe)	W.B.Cousins (cafe)	Mrs.A.Cousins	A.Cousins (+tob.)
100.	N.Brindley (fancy/china)	J.B.Hewett (fancy goods)	J.V.Hewett	F.Ayriss (shoe repair)

★ Left hand side looking from Churchill.

	1914	1920	1929	1938
1.	Uxbridge Arms (S. Reece)	S. Reece	S. Reece	J. Clark
3.	J. Clark (hairdresser)	J. Clark	J. Clark	J. Clark
5.	?	R. Edwards (tobacco)	R. Edwards	R. Edwards (wholesale)
7.	M. Biningsley (fruit/fish)	M. Biningsley	?	Harper/Powis (hair)
9.	M. Biningsley (fruit/fish)	M. Biningsley	?	Evans & Co.(estate)+ Thomas/Durrell(sol.)
11.	T.S. Paddock (leather)	T.S. Paddock (boot/saddle)		C. Gooders (shoes)
13.		EMPTY SPACE		W. Elliott (fish/fruit)
15.		Ball & Rigby (tailors)	J. Ball (tailor)	?
17.		G. Smith	EMPTY SPACE	
19.			EMPTY SPACE	
21.		EMPTY SPACE	S. Smith (doctor)	J.G. Stooke (doctor)
23.		EMPTY SPACE	H. Ball (men's clothes)	Ferneyhough (acc.) +Ferneyhough (account)
25.		EMPTY SPACE		H. Ball (outfitters)
27.		EMPTY SPACE		
29.		EMPTY SPACE		
31.	J. Ball	J. Ball		
33.	G. Smith(draper)	G. Smith		Moreton/Bullock
35.	Post Office(J. Woodcock)	Post Office(F. Wilson)	P.O. (F. Wilson)	P.O.
37.	Martyn's Stores	Co-op Society	Co-op Society	Co-op Society
39.	P. Rosa (confect.)	J. Rogers (cafe/confect.)	?	?
41.	J. Bird (hair)	J. Bird	J. Bird	J. Bird
43.	J. Bray (fancy)	J. Bray	J. Bray	Hames(cycle/radio)
45.	B. Sowter (tailor)	F.W. Smithyman(tailor)	S.E. Walker	S.E. Walker + Collins(shoe repairs)
47.	A. Ayriss	R. Harvey(bootmaker)	?	?

	1914	1920	1929	1938
49.				
51.	G.T. Mason(grocer)	G.T. Mason	G.T. Mason	G.T. Mason
53.	R. Moore	J. Cope (stationer)	J. Cope(news/printer)	J. Willis(newsagent)
55.	F. Summers(draper)	S. Taylor(baker)	S. Taylor	S. Taylor
57.	J. Pope (fried fish)	J. Pope	Moreton/Bullock (tailor/milliner)	?
59.	A. Edwards(grocer)	A. Edwards	A. Edwards	A. Edwards
61.	G. Goscombe(boots)	E. Goscombe	Craners (clothiers)	Piano/furniture
63.		Eastman's Ltd. (butcher)	Eastmans	?
65.	Neale's Tea Stores +	Neale's Tea Stores	Pearkes	Pearkes
67.	Lloyd's Bank	Lloyd's Bank	Lloyd's Bank	Lloyd's Bank
69.	Eastman (butcher)	T.H. Webster (photos)	Barclay's Bank	Barclay's Bank
71.	Ball & Rigby (m.cloth)	W. Webster (butcher)	S. Stanton(butcher)	S. Stanton
73.	Martyn (chemist)			
75.	S. Stanton (confect)	S. Stanton	S. Stanton	Stammers Ltd.
77.	Moore's Factory	Moore's	Moore's	?
	Anglesey Hotel – landlords:-			
	J.W. Bennett	J.W. Bennett	S.Reece	M.Martin
101.	Rhodes (stationer)	H. Rhodes	?	?
101a.				G. Shepherd (plum)
101c.				C. Moreton (shoes)
103.	Rhodes (milliner)	?	Craner/Watwood (tob.)	F. Beresford (gen.)
105.	W. Deakin	W. Deakin		R. Jones
107.	F.G. Sellman (cycles)	F.G. Sellman	?	T.H. Wood
109.	W. Seelhoff	W. Seelhoff		
111.	J. Johnson	J. Johnson	Johnson (dyers)	J.W. Whitehouse

Appendix 2

OCCUPANTS OF MARKET STREET 1953

★Right hand side looking from Churchill.

2.	Bon Marche (drapery, fancy goods) E.Clarke		52a.	E.M. Griffiths (weddings/birthdays)
4.	?		54.	Lavender (draper)
6.	J. Clarke (ladies hairdresser)		56.	Melias (grocer)
	Advertising hoarding		58.	Carter
			60.	Dewhurst (butcher)
12.	A. Peake (furniture)		62.	V.R. Hewitt (hardware)
14.	A. Peake (furniture)		64.	R.F. Houlston (grocer/florist)
16.	Tranter (butchers)		66.	J. Bradbury (tobacco/sweets)
18.	W.H. Holmes (greengrocer/fish)		68.	Levine (half price store)
20.	A. Tribali (cafe/ice cream parlour)		68a.	Mesdames Keen (ladies outfitters)
22.	(Cross lived here)		72.	Foster Bros. (men's clothing)
24.	Hollands (clothing)		74.	F. Haycock (butcher)
26.	W.G. Webb (jewels/watches)		76/78	H.E. Hall (antiques)
28.	Frisby (shoes)		80.	Hednesford Advertiser
30.	W.H. Elsmore (fish & chips)		84.	Midland Bank
32.	G. Merritt (butcher)		86.	Market Hall
34.	Co-op Stores		88.	S. Lowe (cafe)
36.	Williams (dentist)		90.	Market Hall
38.	B.A. Hardwick (grocers)		92.	Bailey Bros.
40.	Progressive Club		94.	Ives (outdoor beer licence)
42.	Printcraft Press		+ 94a.	Nocks (corn/seeds)
44.	E.J. Merrett (wool)		96.	L. Williams (chemist)
46.	Maypole (grocers)		98.	A. Bagley (tobacco/sweets)
48.	Collins (shoes)		100.	J. Jones (ladies hairdresser)
50.	R. Whittle (chemist)			*★On the right hand side of the bridge
52.	Johnson (laundry/cleaners)			Civic Restaurant and Dando's warehouse

★Left hand side.

1.	Les Clarke (hairdresser)
3.	Registry Office
5.	Edwards (tobacco/sweets)
7.	?
9.	? (Glovers lived here)
11.	? (Goodess lived here)
13.	?
15.	?
17.	?
19.	Elliots (greengrocer/florist)
21.	Dr. John G. Stooke (Lowlands House)
23/25.	Howard Ball (men's clothing)
23/25a.	First floor – V. Tennant (ladies hair)
27.	?
29.	?
31.	Owen (shoes)
33.	?
35.	Moreton & Bullock (ladies outfitters)
37.	Post Office
39.	?
41.	R. Andrews (gift shop)
43.	Hames Bros. (radio, T.V. & cycles)
45.	Co-op stores (drapery/tailoring)

Eskrett Street

49.	Lichfield City Laundry
51.	G. Mason (grocer)
53.	T. Willis (Olsens lived here)
55.	S. Taylor (baker/confectionery)
57.	L. West (fruit & veg.)
59.	Moreton (grocer)
61/63	Central piano and furnishing salon
65.	Valeting service
67.	Tennants/Wimbush (baker)
69.	Lloyd's Bank
71.	Stanton (butcher)
73.	Stanton (confectioner)
75.	Joseph Lucas Factory
101.	Moreton (shoe repairs)
101a.	G.E. Shepherd (painter/decorator)
101b.	R. Bailey (fish & chips)
103.	S. Jones (newsagent)
105.	Morris (Army/Navy)

★On the left hand side of the bridge.

Griffiths (butcher)

Cartwright (shoes)

Hardman (hardware)